ROUGH NOTES
OF THE
CAMPAIGN
IN
SINDE AND AFFGHANISTAN
IN 1838–9

BEING EXTRACTS FROM A PERSONAL
JOURNAL KEPT WHILE ON THE
STAFF OF THE ARMY OF THE INDUS

BY MAJOR JAMES OUTRAM
23d. REGT N.I.
NOW POLITICAL AGENT IN SINDE.

The Naval & Military Press Ltd

Published by
The Naval & Military Press Ltd
Unit 10 Ridgewood Industrial Park,
Uckfield, East Sussex,
TN22 5QE England
Tel: +44 (0) 1825 749494
Fax: +44 (0) 1825 765701
www.naval-military-press.com

In reprinting in facsimile from the original, any imperfections are inevitably reproduced and the quality may fall short of modern type and cartographic standards.

PREFATORY NOTICE.

CIRCUMSTANCES have induced me to consent to the printing of the following rough notes from my journal during the late Campaign in Sinde and Affghanistan. I presume not to attempt a narrative of the great Military operations, or to describe minutely the countries and people which our arms have subdued. All this I leave to abler authors, whose works will, I doubt not, in due time, be submitted to the judgment, and for the information of the public, while this volume, which consists chiefly of personal details, has been printed simply for the perusal of those valued friends, to whom it will be PRESENTED, and to whom it is accordingly OFFERED as a token of my thankfulness for the warm and continued interest which they have evinced in my proceedings during the period I served in the Army of the Indus. With the view of illustrating my journal, and to compensate in some measure for its barrenness in details of general interest, I have directed the chief public papers referring to the Campaign, to be embodied in an Appendix.

J. O.

BOMBAY, *March*, 1840.

TABLE OF CONTENTS.

CHAPTER		Page
I.	Sinde	1
II.	Sinde—Tatta	12
III.	The Ameers of Sinde	20
IV.	Sinde—The Indus—Hyderabad	28
V.	Sinde. The submission of the Ameers	38
VI.	Sehwan—The Arrul River	42
VII.	Shah Shooja ool Moolk—Upper Sinde	48
VIII.	Upper Sinde—Cutch Gundava	56
IX.	Cutch Gundava—Dadur	64
X.	The Bolan Pass	71
XI.	Affghanistan—Candahar	79
XII.	Candahar	88
XIII.	March from Candahar to Ghizni	98
XIV.	The Storm of Ghizni	108
XV.	The Pursuit of Dost Mahommed Khan	119
XVI.	The Pursuit—Continued	125
XVII.	The Escape of Dost Mahommed Khan	131
XVIII.	Operations against the Ghiljees	141
XIX.	Operations against the Ghiljees —Continued	149
XX.	Advance upon Khelat	158
XXI.	Capture of Khelat	164
XXII.	Journey from Khelat to Sonmeanee	170
XXIII.	Journey Continued	177
XXIV.	Arrival at Sonmeanee	183
XXV.	Conclusion.—Letter from the Envoy and Minister at Cabul	190
APPENDIX.		195

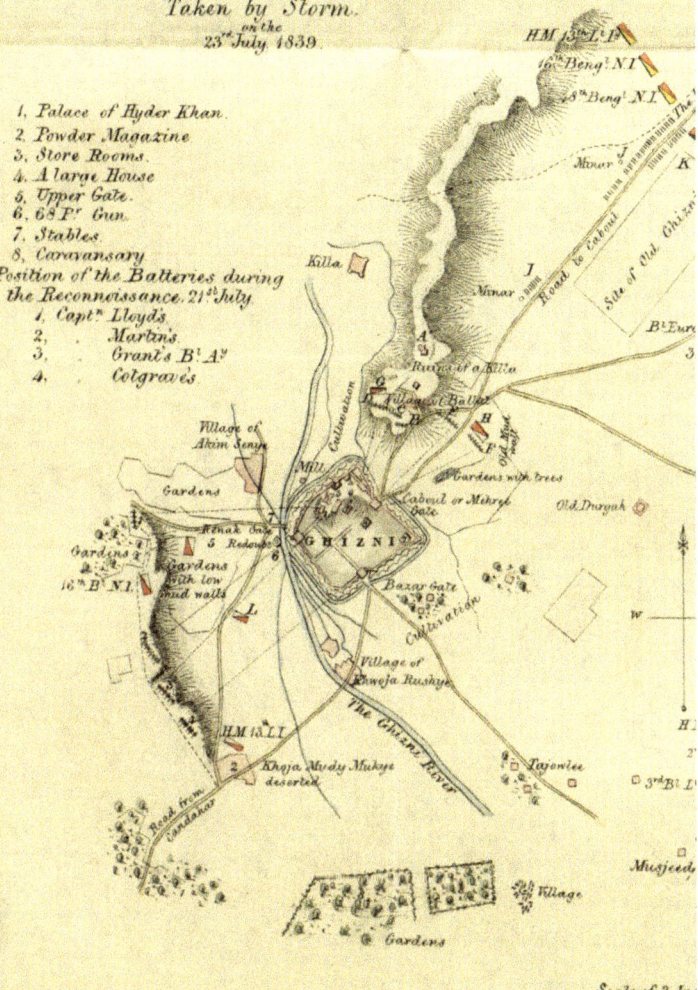

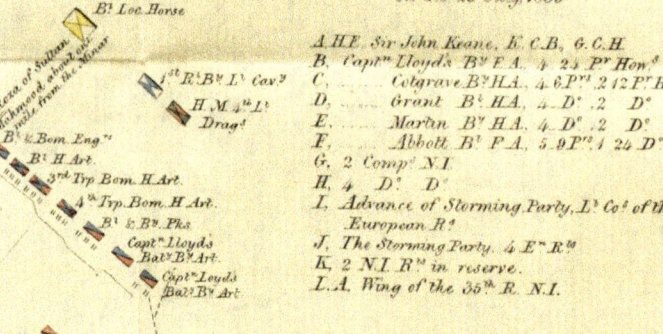

REFERENCES
to
The Storm of Ghizni,
On the 23rd July, 1839

A. H.E. Sir John Keane, K.C.B, G.C.H.
B. Captⁿ Lloyd's B^y F.A. 4 24 Pr How^s
C. ...... Cotgrave B^y H.A. 4 6 P^{rs}. 2 12 P^r H^s
D. ...... Grant B^y H.A. 4 D°. 2 D°
E. ...... Martin B^y H.A. 4 D°. 2 D°
F. ...... Abbott B^y F.A. 5 9 P^{rs}. 1 24 D°
G. 2 Comp^s N.I.
H. 4 D°. D°.
I. Advance of Storming Party. L^t Co^s of the European R^t
J. The Storming Party. 4 Eⁿ R^{ts}
K. 2 N.I. R^{ts} in reserve.
L.A. Wing of the 35th R. N.I.

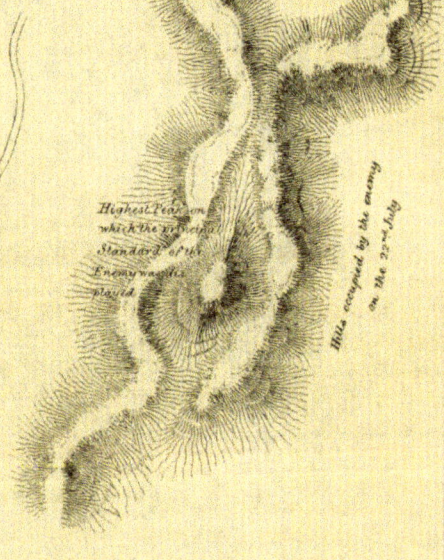

ches to a Mile

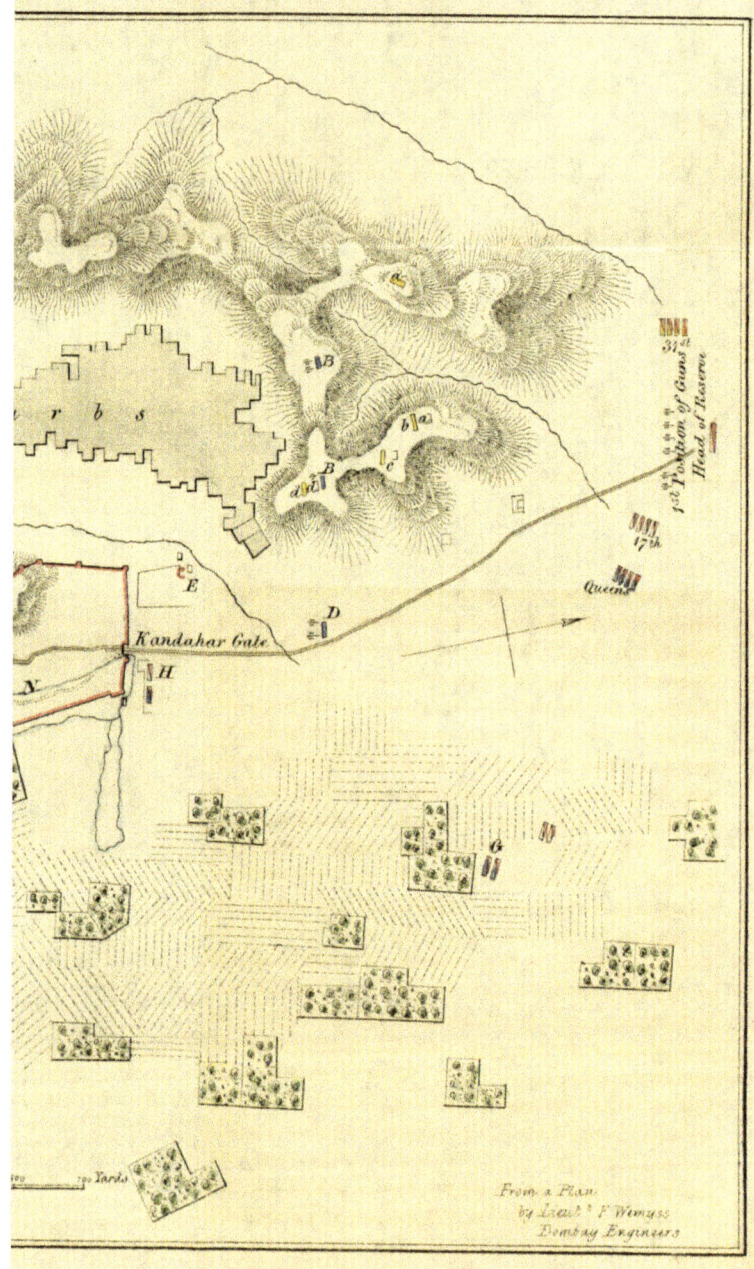

ERRATUM.

Page 52, 10*th line, for* " thousand" *read* " hundred"

ROUGH NOTES

OF THE

CAMPAIGN

IN

SINDE AND AFFGHANISTAN.

CAMPAIGN

IN

SINDE AND AFFGHANISTAN,

IN 1838—39.

CHAPTER I.

SINDE.

HAVING been permitted to volunteer for service, during the approaching Campaign, which has for its object the restoration of Shah Shooja ool Moolk to the throne of Cabul, and being appointed Extra Aid-de-Camp to Lieut.-General Sir John Keane, K. C. B., G. C. H., I embarked on the 21st November, 1838, on board the Semiramis steamer, at Bombay, with His Excellency and suite.—22d. Delayed in the middle ground till 2 P. M. for new hawsers to replace others carried away in towing our convoy, the Taptee brig, and two boats.—27th. In the morning passed the Hannah and Syden, transports, and at midday anchored off the Hujamree mouth of the Indus. Found Major-General Willshire and a portion of the first Brigade already there, also Her Majesty's 18-gun brig Cruizer, the Company's brig of war Palinurus, and the schooner Constance.—28th. A portion of the troops sent up the river to the encamping ground near Vikkur, twenty miles. Lieutenant Eastwick, Assistant to Colonel Pottinger, Resident in Sinde, arrived from thence, representing that no preparations whatever had been made by the Ameers of Sinde for transporting the troops, or provisioning them.—29th. Dispatched by the Commander-in-Chief, in the Constance schooner, on a mission to Cutch, to procure assistance in land and water carriage.—30th. Boarded two horse boats belonging to the Horse Artillery.

1st December. Anchored at midnight off Mandavie.—2d. Landed in the morning, and found Captain Ward, one of the Resident's Assistants, at the Palace; arranged with him for the dispatch to the Army of boats, forage, and sheep; in the evening left for Bhooj; travelled there on camels and horseback.—3d. Arrived at Bhooj at daybreak, forty miles: arranged with Captain Melville, Assistant Resident in charge, for the supply of five hundred additional camels, five hundred having already been sent off viâ Luckput, and four hundred pack bullocks to be shipped at Mandavie. Visited the Rao at noon to convey Sir John Keane's remembrances and good wishes, and received cordial messages from His Highness in reply. In the evening departed on return to Mandavie.—4th. Breakfasted with Captain Ward at Mandavie; found that twenty-two boats had been dispatched the day before with forage and sheep; engaged more boats for the conveyance of pack bullocks, and to tow the Mootnee Indus boat, which, as she was lying useless at Mandavie, I took upon myself to place in requisition. Sailed in the evening.—5th. Passed the anchorage off the Hujamree, but not in sight.—6th. At sunset anchored off Curachee, a port in Sinde, sixty miles north-west of the Hujamree mouth.

7th. In the evening went on shore in a native boat, without servants or baggage of any kind, having sent back the Constance to the Hujamree, determining myself to go overland to camp, and hoping to excite confidence by displaying it in thus going totally unattended,—my object being ostensibly merely to look after camels, but in reality also to feel the temper of the natives, and to endeavour to ascertain the actual intentions of their rulers. Put up in the house of a wealthy Banian, whom I knew to be in our interests.—The Hakim (Governor) of Curachee, hearing of my arrival, intimated his expectation that I should visit him, but I answered that as I was the representative of the British General, he must come to me if he wished to see me. He came accordingly to inquire my object, and I replied, that it was to see whether the collection of camels, as promised by the Ameers, was really in progress: found, however, after much conversation, that no such directions had been given by the Ameers, but that a friendly Banian, named

Nao-Mull, had gone in person to Gharry-Kote, half way to the British camp, to exert his influence in our behalf: gave the Hakim to understand that I should acquaint Colonel Pottinger with his masters' falsehood, and informed him that their backwardness in affording aid must turn to their own disadvantage, by detaining the force so much longer in their country, or by compelling us to help ourselves; that our immediate object was to join the Bengal Army at Shikarpore, and that it obviously was the interest of the Sinde Government to facilitate our advance.

8th. The principal inhabitants called together by the Hakim, to consult what was to be done in consequence of my presence, and the communication I had made; and also to deliberate on a letter received last night from the Ameers, stating that the sirdars dispatched by them to the British camp, to compliment the Commander-in-Chief, had there received information, that forty thousand troops were about to follow the present force for the purpose of forcibly occupying Sinde. It appeared they were much puzzled how to act, and one of the party was deputed to question me in the hope of ascertaining our real intentions: I confined my conversation with him, however, to a simple denial of the report that forty thousand men were coming, reiterating my injunctions to expedite the collection of the necessary carriage. The public consultation terminated at last in a resolution not to molest our agent in his exertions to procure camels, although it was decided that no aid was to be given him without orders from the Ameers. Nao-Mull's brother subsequently succeeded in collecting a few camels on the spot, and dispatched his emissaries to engage others, expecting in two or three days to complete about three hundred at Curachee, which I directed to be sent after me without delay.

9th. Departed soon after midnight from Curachee, accompanied by Sookram, one of Nao-Mull's brothers, he and his servant, and a camel-man and myself mounted on two camels. About 4 A. M. it became so cold as to compel us to dismount and spread our beds in the jungle till the sun rose, when we resumed our journey, and travelled till midday; then dismounted for half-an-hour to rest the camels, which were miserable brutes. In the evening arrived at Gharry-Kote, where I found Nao-Mull surrounded by Beloche camel drivers, whom he was endeavouring to persuade to join the English. He was much surprised to see a British officer, no warning having been given him of my approach, but immediately took advantage of my presence to appeal to me for confirmation of the terms he had promised to the camel-men, which I at once assured them would be scrupulously fulfilled by the Commander-in-Chief. On receiving this assurance, they declared themselves satisfied, and expressed their determination to join the British camp immediately. Accordingly, they left that night for the purpose, with three hundred camels, two hundred more being expected by Nao-Mull next day.

The road from Curachee to Gharry-Kote is a sandy plain almost the whole way, generally perfectly bare, but occasionally varied by tamarisk jungle.

bordering the dry beds of rivers, which are filled only in the rains, although water can be obtained in them by digging a foot or two deep in the sand. The sea is visible nearly the whole way. A branch of the Indus runs past Gharry-Kote, navigable up to that place, but not beyond it for boats of considerable size. The distance from Curachee I should estimate at about forty miles, having occupied our camels nearly twelve hours, at an average pace of about three-and-a-half miles per hour. About half way is a low stony range of undulating ground, scattered with Mahomedan tombs, over a distance of two miles, and said to be the remains of a Mahomedan camp, of which I found no other traces. The tombs were very numerous, and generally well constructed of cut stone, but of small size. At about two miles from Gharry-Kote, I went off the road a few hundred yards to inspect the ruins of a city covering a low hill; edging the river for about a quarter of a mile, the foundations of walls, bastions, and houses, can be distinctly traced, and appear very ancient. Coins are frequently washed up in the rains: the name given by my guide was 'Bamboora.'

Late at night I was visited by the brother, Kumr Ali, of a chief, styled Meer Ali, the Jam of the tribe of Jokeas, whose possessions are held on the tenure of furnishing twelve thousand fighting men to the state in times of war. After some general conversation in the usual style,* my visitor whispered to

* "The propensity of the Sindian courtiers to flatter strangers, and even each other, is ludicrous to a European. Scarcely two persons of the higher rank ever met together

me that, understanding I was an officer in the confidence of the British General, he was anxious to make a certain secret communication, and that he proposed leaving with me a person in his confidence for that purpose until all others should have withdrawn. The chief's Deewan, or Secretary, waited accordingly, and when all the rest were gone, showed me certain documents bearing the seals of the Ameers, and of considerable importance, as displaying their real intentions and treachery. These were offered for the inspection of Colonel Pottinger on certain conditions, with permission to that gentleman to copy them after ascertaining their authenticity; the chief giving as a cause for his faithlessness to his sovereigns, that he had been despoiled and injured by the present dynasty. To this communication I merely gave answer, that I should see Colonel Pottinger next day, when I would communicate the chief's wish and information.

10th. At 6 A. M. left Gharry-Kote, and travelled without any intermission till 9 P. M., a distance of forty-five miles, estimating an average of about three miles per hour; the camels latterly being completely knocked up, and one of them giving in about three miles from camp, and not overtaking us till next day. This day the whole route lay across the Delta of the Indus, being generally covered with tamarisk jungle of the most luxurious growth, and with another

in my presence, without bespattering each other with the most fulsome compliments, and both joining in exalting me to the skies by the most far-fetched and hyperbolic praises."
—*Dr. Burnes' Visit to Sinde.*

shrub, a most favourite food for camels, which are seen grazing on it in great numbers. The country is intersected by dry artificial canals every three or four hundred yards, which I was informed had had no water in them for the last three or four years, in consequence of one of the branches of the Indus which supplied them having altered its course. At about ten miles from Gharry-Kote, and opposite to a small village called Meerpore, the ruins of a city were pointed out to me some distance off the road, which I had not time to visit; it is called 'Moujdurria,' and said to be Mahomedan, of much greater extent and in better preservation than Bamboora.*

At about thirty miles distance from Gharry-Kote, passed the 'Bogaur' branch of the Indus, a stream running at the rate of about three miles an hour, four

* It is probable that these ancient cities, and also the one subsequently mentioned on the 28th January, are the same as those referred to by Dr. Burnes in the first portion of the following extract. The town of Meerpoor, which he mentions, is different from that referred to in the text, and on the eastern side of the Indus. "From a similar change in the course of the Indus, the ancient cities of Debal Sindy, which occupied a site between Kurachee and Tatta, and of Braminabad or Kullan Kote, which was near the latter place, were also deserted, although at what date it is difficult to surmise, leaving scarcely a wreck behind. At Shahkapoor, a populous village in the vicinity of Meerpoor, are still to be seen the remains of an extensive fort and city, said to have been the residence of Dahooda Rai, the last of the Soomra Princes, who flourished about the year one thousand and three hundred of our era. The bricks which form part of these ruins are of large dimensions, measuring twenty inches by eight."—*Visit to Sinde.*

hundred yards broad, and up to the camel's girth at low water, the tide there appearing to rise about two or three feet: passed many villages—generally small hamlets. On this day's route, there was also considerable cultivation, principally of sugar cane, and an oil plant, the latter highly enjoyed by camels. At about four miles from the cantonment of our army, which is situated on the Hujamree mouth of the Indus, near Vikkur, or, as it is called, Ghorabaree, and about twenty miles above the anchorage at the river's mouth, the tamarisk jungle ceases, and the country becomes quite open, and pretty well cultivated, being intersected by numerous canals supplied by the Hujamree.

The road from Curachee to our camp may be estimated at about ninety-five miles; it could only be passed by small detachments of troops, owing to the scarcity of water in some parts, especially the first portion of the road; at this season, no grass or forage whatever for horses or cattle is to be found, although I was told that there is no scarcity in usual seasons. Judging from the remains of deserted towns and dry canals, the country appears to have fallen from a state of much greater prosperity than it now enjoys: this is attributed to the despotic government of the Ameers, which encourages neither trade nor manufactures, and the populace appeared by no means sorry to hail the arrival of Englishmen among them, except when in the presence of the Beloche officials, before whom they dared not display any such feeling. The latter would willingly have given evidence of their dislike to us, had they not been uncertain what course the Ameers intended to pursue, and therefore feared to commit them. On the whole, however, I had no great incivility to complain of, and experienced no difficulties of any consequence in passing through the country. The luxuriant tamarisk jungles, covering the great portion of the Delta, would afford an inexhaustible supply of excellent fuel for steamers, should they be established on the Indus.

11th. Inspected the camp, which occupies a space of upwards of a mile in length, and half as much in breadth, its rear being protected by the river, and the front flanks by canals containing good water: found all the troops assembled, except the 1st Cavalry, Auxiliary Horse, and a portion of the Grenadiers. Few of the Dragoon horses had arrived, however, and none of the artillery stores are yet brought up from the anchorage,—casualties since the troops left Bombay being four or five Europeans, and about twenty horses, sixteen of the latter having been lost in a boat wrecked on the bar. The camp healthy.—12th to 14th. Landing stores, the Grenadier Regiment, and the Dragoon horses, which are now complete.

15th. Nao-Mull arrived in camp, accompanied by Kumr Ali: says he has prepared in all one thousand camels: those from Cutch have not yet arrived, owing to the refusal of the Ameer of Meerpore to allow them to pass, and they are consequently coming on by a more circuitous route. The information received through Nao-Mull confirms the report of the Ameers' preparations for resistance, should certain stipulations be insisted on, which are to be enforced on the arrival of the army at the capital.—17th. An officer of the Hyderabad Government brought in the very camels engaged by Nao-Mull, which he had seized in the outskirts of the camp, whither they were being brought in accordance with the engagement entered into with Nao-Mull, whereas the Hyderabad agent wished it to be understood that they had been procured through the exertions of the Ameers. This is the first instance of the servants of these princes even affecting to assist us in any way, although they themselves have been most profuse in their professions of earnest endeavours to aid us.

CHAPTER II.

SINDE—TATTA.

19th. The long-expected camels from Cutch arrived, having been delayed by the refusal of the chief of Meerpore, a subject and relative of the Ameers, to allow them a passage through his territory. This chief, whose hostility to the English is notorious and his boast, has, by this and other unfriendly acts, rendered himself amenable to punishment, which he will doubtless bring hereafter upon himself from the Reserve Force, he being too insignificant to require the detention of our army for his chastisement. The hostile preparations of the Ameers, who, whilst they continue to profess the utmost friendship for us, are levying *en masse* their fighting men from the age of seventeen to sixty, bringing their guns from Larkhana to Hyderhabad, &c. &c., render it imperative that the communications of our army should be maintained by a strong force stationed in Sinde, even should we pass through the country without actual rupture with them : accordingly, the Resident this day dispatched an express requisition for the Reserve Force, which had previously been warned, to be assembled as early as practicable at Curachee. It will consist in the first instance of H. M 's 40th Foot, the 2nd Grenadiers, and 26th Regt. N. I., one company of European Artillery, and one company of Golundauze. Another native Regiment is to be sent to Vikkur, and the addition of a Cavalry Regiment and Troop of Horse Artillery, recommended by Sir John Keane, awaits a reference to the Governor-General.

24th. Being now sufficiently equipped with carriage to enable us to advance by Brigades, while the heavy stores go up the Indus in flat-bottomed boats, protected by gun boats manned by the Indian Navy, and all the troops being now assembled except the Irregular Horse, and a portion of the 1st Cavalry and Artillery, the Commander-in-Chief determined to advance to Tatta, and the preparations having been completed by this day, we had accordingly the pleasure to depart from Vikkur, of which place we were heartily tired.

The first division, consisting of the 2nd Brigade of Infantry, composed of H. M.'s 17th, and the 19th, and 23rd Regiments, N. I., two squadrons of the 4th Dragoons, the 3rd Troop of Horse Artillery, and a company of Foot Artillery, with Sir John Keane and the Head Quarters' Staff, marched at 7 A. M. The road for the first five miles lay over a sterile plain, with a few wretched villages at great intervals in the distance, and then entered a thick tamarisk jungle, which continued to our halting ground. A pontoon bridge had been laid across the 'Jug,' a tributary stream of the Chagloo, about thirty yards broad, and impracticable for artillery, from the depth of mud. The camp was pitched between the 'Merwa' and 'Jug,' both streams joining just below the pontoon bridge, and flowing into the 'Chagloo' branch of the Indus, distant about half a mile.

25th December. Marched at half-past six A. M. to Somana Kote, nine miles. Sir John Keane declared himself highly pleased with the appearance, order, and regularity of the several corps on the line of march, and issued a memorandum expressive of his satisfaction, in which he styled the demeanour of the troops worthy of veterans. The first part of the road this day was over a plain affording scanty pasture, but with hardly a vestige of cultivation. The last four miles were partially covered with tamarisk jungle, and the road was as smooth as possible the whole way: our camp was pitched close to a grove of baubul trees of great size, the first we had seen in Sinde. Here the cholera made its appearance in the 19th Regiment N. I.: of eight cases, which have occurred during the day, two have proved fatal, and three of the others appear to be hopeless.

26th. Marched at sunrise for Gholam Shah Ke Got, seventeen miles. Two of the cholera patients died during the night, but no new cases have appeared. The first nine miles of our road lay over a barren plain of fine white sand, which rose in such clouds as entirely to obscure the column. About eight miles from camp we entered a dense tamarisk jungle, and, by some mistake, no men having been left to point out the road which had been cleared by the pioneers, the head of the column pursued a wrong path for some distance, until the artillery, finding the route no longer practicable, had to countermarch, and the whole line being thus thrown out, the troops did not reach their ground till past two o'clock. The men were much jaded, and suffered greatly from want of water, of which there was none to be found the whole way. No new cases of cholera. Camp pitched on the right bank of the Bogaur branch of the Indus, formerly the main stream, but now choked up by sand banks.* In the course of the day all stragglers were brought up on camels, which had been sent back with water for the purpose of assisting them.

27th. Sir John Keane considered it advisable to halt, in order to recruit the camels, which are quite unequal to their work, although generally not carrying more than a third of the load of camels in India. This was a most disagreeable day, the wind blowing a gale and very cold, while the dust was so thick as to render it impossible to see to the distance of a few yards. The village of Gholam Shah is the best

* The site of Tatta, it would appear from Mahomedan historians, was scarcely peopled, and utterly unproductive at the time of the Arab conquest, and even until the change in the course of the river had supplied that part of Sinde with water; but it is useless to indulge in surmises, and were anything wanting to prove the utter futility of speculating on such a subject, it is the fact, that the great western branch below Tatta, the Mehran of Rennell, and the modern "Bogaur," which was described to be the main river when I visited Tatta in January 1828, was scarcely knee deep at the same season three years afterwards, and not in existence at all when Mr. Heddle was collecting materials for his report to Government in the beginning of 1836.—*Dr. Burnes' Visit to Sinde.*

we have yet seen; a large quantity of sugar-cane is cultivated in its neighbourhood, as well as on the opposite side of the river, where there is another considerable village. The fields here, and indeed throughout all that portion of Sinde which I have yet seen, are irrigated by the Persian wheel, worked by camels.

28th. To Tatta 12 miles—marched at sun-rise, the artillery detained three hours at the commencement, in consequence of one of the guns with its six horses being swamped in a quicksand when passing the edge of the river. After great labour, all were extricated without damage. Our road this day was quite a contrast to the sandy plains we had hitherto passed, and lay over undulating stony hills covered with prickly pear bushes, giving to the country an aspect very similar to the Deccan between Seroor and Ahmednuggur. About three miles from Tatta we passed the remains of a strong and extensive fortress.—Its founder and history could not be learnt with any degree of accuracy, but it is said to be eight hundred years old. The Indus once flowed past the rocky range on which the fort stands, but it has now receded six miles to the eastward of its old channel.

Our camp was pitched about a mile from the town, with a range of low stony hills on our rear, extending to a considerable distance in a northerly direction. Several small tanks afford a supply of water, and are the remains of the annual inundation of the Indus, which then covers our encamping ground, as well as the whole of the plain surrounding Tatta, the city itself having but little perceptible elevation above it. The heights behind camp are covered with tombs and other Mahomedan remains. Some of the former are very extensive and in good preservation, being not inferior in ornament to the best I have seen in India. Some of the domes especially are covered with beautiful lackered work, formed by glazed tiles and bricks, inscribed all over with sentences from the Koran. Several Persian epitaphs, copied by Captain Sidney Powell, proved to be from two hundred to two hundred and fifty years old.

29th. The coldest day I have ever experienced in the east—the thermometer never above 62° in the tents, and a bitter cold North-Easterly wind bringing with it intolerable dust, of so impalpable a nature, that it is impossible to exclude it. I rode with Sir John Keane to the Indus. It flows about four miles to the Eastward of the city, and appeared to me to be nearly a mile broad, and very shoal, being nowhere above two or three fathoms deep. The water is extremely muddy, and the banks at this part are perfectly desolate. Altogether, the classic Indus has here the most uninviting appearance. In passing through the town, we visited the Jumma Musjid, which incloses a quadrangle of about sixty yards square, and is built on the plan of a Persian caravanserai. Some of the principal domes and recesses of this building are most beautifully lackered, the patterns resembling fine mosaic of brilliant colors. The mosque is in a very dilapidated state, and fast falling to ruin.*

* "With the exception of the Jumma Musjid, or great

The town of Tatta, which was founded A. D. 1485, is in a wrecked condition, and from being populous and rich beyond any other city in this part of the world, has now scarcely twelve thousand inhabitants, its trade being entirely destroyed by the narrow policy of the Ameers. Under a fostering Government, however, it might soon recover its former prosperity, as it is most advantageously situated for trade. At a distance, Tatta has a very imposing appearance, but on a nearer approach the illusion vanishes —its houses, although sometimes three stories high, are built of wattle and mud, white-washed, with terrace roofs; the streets are narrow and intricate, but not so filthy as might be expected: the natives are dirty, and generally squalid.

30th. General Willshire, with the 1st Brigade of Infantry and Captain Ward's Horse, joined the army, having lost only one man by cholera. The disease seems to have disappeared from our camp, after having carried off altogether eight of the 19th Regiment, and four or five camp followers. 31st. Sir John Keane examined the neighbourhood, in search of a favourable site for a cantonment for the subsidiary force which it is contemplated to establish here, and His Excellency selected the table land on the

Mahomedan temple for the assemblage of true believers at Tatta, and the tombs of the Caloras, and Talpoors at the capital, there are no modern edifices either indicating taste or durability, in Sinde. The former was erected so late as the reign either of Shah Jehan, or of Aurungzebe, and by one of these sovereigns; but it is already a gloomy dilapidated building, in which 'the moping owl doth to the bat complain.' "—*Visit to Sinde; by J. Burnes, K. H.*

hills in rear of camp. The camels which had been obtained in Sinde with so much difficulty, being required to return to Vikkur for stores, &c., their owners positively refused to move: at last, however, three hundred only, out of one thousand five hundred engaged in our service, were persuaded to go. At least two thousand camels must be purchased immediately, in addition to about one thousand Cutch and private camels now with us, to enable us to reach Shikarpore; beyond which place, when deprived of our water carriage, ten thousand camels will at least be required for the Bombay army alone. How they are to be procured in addition to those that will be required for the Bengal Army, which Sir Alexander Burnes cannot equip, notwithstanding that he has swept the whole country in our advance, remains to be seen.

An express from that officer, just received, announces that the Khyrpore chief has come entirely into our views, and has made over the fortress of Bukkur to us. The Ameers of Hyderabad are now to all appearance frightened out of their doughty resolves to resist us, and are dispersing the rabble which they had assembled at the capital by their levy *en masse*. Report says, that the Candahar Chiefs have fled from the capital, and that they, as well as Dost Mahommed Khan, have tendered their submission; in which case, whilst our great preparations will lead to no warfare, our march is likely to terminate at Shikarpore.

CHAPTER III.

THE AMEERS OF SINDE.

[It appears advisable that I should here introduce, for the benefit of those friends in Europe who may read this journal, some information regarding the Ameers of Sinde, whom I have occasion so frequently to mention, and who, for many years past, have occupied so prominent a place in all proceedings connected with the countries bordering on the river Indus. This I shall abridge from the account given of those Chiefs by my friend Dr. James Burnes, in his "Visit to the Court of Sinde." I quote from the 4th Edition of the work published at Bombay in 1839,* the last English Edition appearing not to contain the Genealogical table of the Talpoors.

'The original Ameers of Sinde were four Chiefs of the Beloche tribe named Talpoor, who established themselves, towards the end of last century, as rulers

* Narrative of a Visit to the Court of the Ameers of Sinde, in 1827-28, by James Burnes, LL. D., F. R. S., Knight of the Guelphic Order, 4th Edit., Bombay, 1839.

of the country, by the expulsion of the previous dynasty of the Caloras, which had held the government for nearly a century previous, as tributaries, successively, to the Delhi Emperors, Nadir Shah, Ahmed Shah Douranee, and his son. The eldest and principal of these Ameers, Futteh Ali Khan, whose bravery and perseverance had been chiefly instrumental in effecting the change, was by the general voice called to the direction of affairs, and was shortly afterwards confirmed as ruler of the country, by the patent of the king of Cabul, Timour Shah. On his own elevation, this prince admitted, to a participation in his high destiny, his three younger brothers, Gholam Ali, Kurm Ali, and Mourad Ali; and the four agreed to reign together, under the denomination of the Ameers, or Lords of Sinde. While they all lived, the strong and unvarying attachment they evinced for each other, gained them the honourable appellation of the *Char Yar*, or the four friends.

'Meer Futteh Ali died in 1801, Gholam Ali in 1811, Kurm Ali in 1828, and Mourad Ali in 1833. The only one of the four, who did not leave male descendants, was Kurm Ali. The present four Ameers are Meers Noor Mahommed, and Mahommed Nusseer Khan, the sons of the late Meer Mourad Ali, and Meers Sobdar Khan, and Mahommed Khan, the sons, respectively, of Meers Futteh Ali Khan, and Gholam Ali Khan. All the reigning chiefs, with the exception of Meer Mahommed Khan, have male children. The different ramifications of the Talpoor family will be best understood by the subjoined Genealogical Table,* in reference to which I have only to remark that the Khypoor Chiefs are the Meers Rustum and Mobaruck; and the Meerpoor prince, Sheer Mahommed, the son of the Ali Mourad, therein mentioned.']

1st. January, 1839. Last night was excessively cold, and the thermometer was said to be down to 35°, though I did not witness it myself. In the afternoon I attended a Durbar, at which the Commander-in-Chief and Colonel Pottinger received a deputation from the Ameers of Sinde, composed of a near relation of theirs, and a representative from each individual Ameer, their professed object being merely to compliment His Excellency on his arrival, but evidently also to seek an explicit declaration of our intentions. After the usual enquiries and con-

* GENEALOGICAL TABLE.

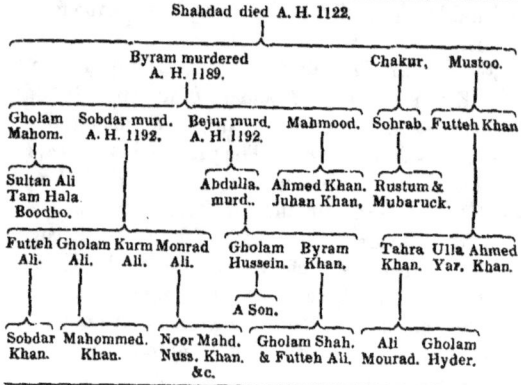

gratulations, they had the assurance to express their hope that their Government had amply assisted us with carriage, and all things necessary, and that their people had zealously served us. They also requested a list of our future intended marches, in order, as they said, that every thing might be prepared at each place for the supply of the force.

In reply to this Colonel Pottinger explicitly stated that no assistance whatever, either in carriage or supplies, had been afforded by the Sinde Government; and that no services had been performed by its officers or people; adding, with respect to the offers to support our troops, that as he had been accustomed to receive similar promises repeatedly from the Ameers, without finding them followed by assistance of any sort, such proffers on the present occasion could not be relied on, were it even customary to accept provisions for our troops gratis, which it never was. It was useless, therefore, he remarked, to consider, or lay down, our marches; all we required being aid in camels, for which we were ready to pay any thing the Ameers should fix, as had been before so repeatedly agreed to. The interview continued nearly an hour, the whole conversation being mere repetitions to the same effect.

Since our arrival here, a large proportion of Nao Mull's camels have deserted, and we are, in consequence, at present totally incapacitated from advancing, and have little prospect of doing so for some time. Many individuals, who have purchased camels, have missed them in the morning, either from their having been stolen, or having made their escape during the night, and if entrusted to natives of Sinde engaged to tend them, they are often carried off when out grazing during the day.—2d. I accompanied Sir John Keane to a lake about seven miles in rear of the camp, where were many Kullum and wild geese, all too wild to be approached. The lake is of no great extent, and is evidently the remains of the annual inundation: the country appeared generally level and covered with tamarisk jungle, and we saw one wretched village about half way. This day and yesterday were hot, but the nights were very cold.

4th. The arrival of the Semiramis steamer at the anchorage reported, bringing the small steamer intended to ply on the Indus, and six hundred coolies for carrying loads,—a most seasonable aid to the Army.—5th. Reports have been received of an inroad by the Meerpoor Chief on Cutch, doubtless at the instigation of the Ameers, to whom he is dependant, although they disclaim all control over him. This diversion they hope will call the attention of this army, and retard its advance. The Beloche army is reported to be re-assembling at the capital. A Beloche placed in confinement for selling liquors to the soldiers, contrary to orders, broke from his guard, and his sword unfortunately having been left in his possession, he attempted to cut his way through the camp, but was shot: luckily he hurt nobody, several cuts he made, at the corporal and his guard, having been warded off by their muskets.

6th, 7th, and 8th. The days are getting warmer, but the nights are still very cold; no intelligence from Hyderabad. 9th. Excessively hot, thermometer upwards of 90°. Accounts from Hyderabad mention that no extraordinary sensation has been produced at the capital, in consequence of the intelligence from the north-westward of leagues against us, which must by this time have reached the Ameers. Their communications, on the contrary, are more humble, and more lavish in professions than heretofore; and appearances would even testify that endeavours are now really being made by their Government to facilitate the advance of the army. These symptoms evince the adoption by the Ameers of a temporising policy in preference to any further attempt to obstruct or check us; the object probably being to see our armies fully occupied by the Affghans—now that there is a reasonable prospect of the latter seriously opposing us—ere they break with us, and then to attempt to expel the troops left in their country; having accomplished which, they may hope to be able to take measures to prevent our return this way. Heretofore, they had feared that the submission of the Affghans to Shah Shooja would leave Sinde at the mercy of the armies about to assemble at Shirkapore, and their only chance, therefore, was to obstruct our advance; but now that there exists a prospect of our being engaged at a distance, they very wisely bid us good speed and send us on.

10th. The first cavalry joined in good order. It has been decided that, while the Army is advancing, Lieutenant Eastwick on behalf of the resident, and myself on the part of the Commander-in-Chief, shall proceed in advance to Hyderabad to tender the treaty. Under present circumstances it is also determined to bring the reserve force to Vikkur instead of landing it at Curachee, with a view of preventing a rupture, since it is supposed that its landing at the latter place would be resisted.

11th. Captain Peat, the Chief Engineer, returned from the surveying route to Curachee. He measured it to be fifty-eight miles, and found the road level, with no obstacle to troops, except a scarcity of water this year, owing to the two last seasons of drought: it is, however, to be found at most places about six or seven feet below the surface, and the soil being everywhere easily dug, an hour or two would suffice to make wells. There is a great scarcity of forage also, in consequence of the unfavorable season, although it is said usually to abound on this road. Captain Peat was not permitted to enter Curachee, which he found jealously guarded, and the Beloche garrison seemed well inclined to quarrel, had he given room for it by attempting to enter the place. He entirely agrees with me in opinion of the absolute necessity of maintaining a depôt at Curachee, to secure the communications of the reserved force, and a detachment also at Gharry Kote; (the same place passed by me, on my route from Curachee to Vikkur,) up to which town a small branch of the Indus is navigable for boats of twenty candies burden. Captain Peat also agrees with me in opinion as to the facility of disembarking and landing stores at Curachee within command of our shipping.

12th. The rear troops of Horse, and company of Foot Artillery joined, so that no troops now remain at Vikkur, except a small guard of Infantry, and Lieutenant Colonel Cunningham's Horse.—13th. It was finally decided that Lieutenant Eastwick and myself should proceed in the Indus steamer to Hyderabad on the 15th or 16th, sending off our baggage to-morrow overland, and timing our departure so as to arrive at the same time as our servants, and thus prevent any appearance of hurry.

CHAPTER IV.

SINDE—THE INDUS—HYDERABAD.

17th Jan. Heavy rain during the night. We embarked on the Indus Steamer in the morning, and started at 10 A. M. Anchored at 7 P. M. off the village of Amrajee Kote, situated on the left bank of the river, and about sixteen miles from Tatta, after having been twice aground and lost about half an hour each time—passing two or three miserable hamlets on both sides of the river. The banks were covered nearly the whole way with dense jungles, enclosed to preserve game for the private amusement of the Ameers, who have thus usurped and laid waste the most fertile portions of the Sinde territory. These jungles overhang the water's edge, and as it is frequently impossible to avoid approaching within pistol-shot, owing to the deep channel running close to them, boats would be at the mercy of an enemy in possession of the Shikargahs, as these hunting forests are termed. Strong parties of infantry would therefore be necessary to flank the river route in case of war, and would be exposed to severe loss in clearing the thickets of opponents.

Unfortunately, the Indus is nowhere wide enough to allow of boats passing out of reach of either side, and it is generally shallow on the side opposite to the Shikargahs.*

18th. Started at 6 A. M., but had to go back some distance to regain the deep channel, and it was half-past 7 before we recovered what we thus lost. Grounded twice, and so lost another hour before midday; afterwards made pretty good way until dark, that is, proceeded at the rate of about 2 miles an hour, beyond which our vessel cannot stem the current with a river boat of coals in tow. Altogether, we may have made about fifteen miles this day. The river banks, for the first five or six miles, con-

---

* "Game restrictions of extraordinary severity are established to guard the aristocratic privileges of the princes; the common people, except in the capacity of beaters for their masters, never being permitted to enter the hunting forests, or to destroy game in their vicinity, under pain of death, a degree of tyranny monstrous even for Sinde, and which would almost exceed belief, did we not know on undoubted authority that the late Meer Futteh Ali Khan, on one occasion, depopulated, at a loss to his revenue of between two and three lacs of rupees annually, one of the most fertile spots in the neighbourhood of Hyderabad, because it was frequented by a species of hog deer, the kota pacha (axis Porcinus), which he had most pleasure in hunting; and that, more recently, Meer Mourad Ali Khan unrelentingly banished the inhabitants of an ancient village, and razed it to the ground, because the crowing of the cocks, and the grazing of the cattle, disturbed the game in his brother's domain, which was contiguous."—*Visit to Sinde, by J. Burnes, K. H.*

tinued of much the same nature as yesterday, becoming afterwards more free from jungle, the river itself wider, and the channel more clear; small stony hills being seen on the right bank, about half way.

19th. We weighed anchor at half-past 6 A. M., and at half-past 10 anchored off Jerk (eight miles), a large village on the right bank, where I landed with Lieutenant Eastwick and walked through the place. The people, being almost entirely Hindoos, were civil. Departed at 12 A. M., and found that, during our absence, the coals had been emptied from the tow boat, which was now cast off, an arrangement by which we gained about a mile an hour. The banks, throughout this day's journey, were quite free from jungle, excepting at two extensive Shikargahs, one on the left bank about half way, and the other on the right, terminating nearly opposite to Hyderabad.

20th. Weighed at daybreak, and passed up the right branch of the Indus, which is here divided into two channels; anchored at 11 A. M. close to Mr. Leckie's tent on the river bank, abreast of Hyderabad, which is about three miles distant. In the afternoon, rode three miles up the river bank in search of a site for bridging, in case the contumacy of the Ameers should oblige us to cross near the capital. A deputation from the Ameers attended to welcome us. 21st. Inspected the fort in the morning, riding close to its walls almost entirely round, and also round the outside of the town.

Artillery would soon breach the fort, which is in itself by no means strong;* the walls are built of brick, on a scarp, generally from twenty to thirty feet in height, but at two places, where the ascent would be obtained by means of the demolished wall, they are not above ten or fifteen feet high. We saw many parties of Beloches encamped within the suburbs, and some thousands are said to be in the fort. Waited till evening, in expectation of being summoned to the durbar, but a frivolous excuse was sent for not seeing us this day, and our attendance was requested at 2 P. M. to-morrow.

22d. At early dawn I again reconnoitred the approaches to the town and fort from every side, and, on passing the Beloche camps, was insulted by abusive language. At 4 P. M. the Ameers sent for us, and received us with much affectation of cordiality. After the usual complimentary speeches, all, excepting confidential attendants, were directed to withdraw, when their Highnesses entered upon the subject of the treaty, a copy of which had been previously furnished to them, and every article of which was commented on : many objections being made, and supported with much plausibility by

* "The city of Hyderabad, as already described, is a collection of wretched low mud hovels, as destitute of the means of defence as they are of external elegance, or internal comfort ; and even the boasted stronghold of the Ameers, which surmounts their capital, is but a paltry erection of ill-burnt bricks, crumbling gradually to decay, and perfectly incapable of withstanding for an hour the attack of regular troops."—*Visit to Sinde ; by J. Burnes, K. H.*

the Ameers, especially by Noor Mahommed Khan. These matters were discussed until sunset, when we were dismissed with every assurance that " the will of the British government was law to that of Sinde," but that a definitive answer could not be given until next day. Meers Noor Mahommed, Nusseer Khan, and Meer Mahommed, were present, the fourth, Sobdar Khan, being on bad terms with the others, was to have been visited separately; but the lateness of the hour obliged us to excuse ourselves from waiting upon his Highness until to-morrow, at a time which has been appointed for him to send for us. In our way to and from the durbar, the streets were thronged with armed Beloches, who looked daggers, and were only restrained from giving vent to their feelings by the presence of the deputation which escorted us. Their numbers are increasing daily: and orders have been issued within the last twenty-four hours, urging the immediate assembly of all fighting men at the capital.

23d. In the morning inspected the hilly ranges situated on the western side of the fort, and thus completed my survey of the place. The hostile intentions of the Ameers are evinced hourly; all supplies to, and communication with, our camp, are prohibited,—and we ascertain that it had been even proposed to attack our little party,—and that an engagement has been solemnly sworn to by all the Ameers and the chiefs, to stand by each other in the approaching struggle. Under these circumstances, and having, moreover, received no communication from the Ameers, or been attended on as appointed, by any one on behalf of Meer Sobdar Khan, we determined to demand either an acceptance of the treaty, or an explicit avowal of their intentions, together with our own dismissal; and, at the same time, to inform the Ameers of the reports that had reached us of their hostile preparations. This message was accordingly sent in the evening, and an immediate answer requested. None was, however, received that night; which circumstance, together with certain hostile indications in our immediate neighbourhood, induced us to be on the alert. About midnight, parties of armed men having been seen to enter the village on our rear, all our servants were immediately put into boats moored outside of a large state-barge aground on the bank, on which all our small detachment of sixty men was formed, with the exception of the sentries, who had orders to retreat on the advance of any body of men. All this was effected silently and quietly, according to previous arrangement, but our preparations having frightened the boatmen, some of them fled, and doubtless communicated our state of readiness to the parties by whom we were beleaguered, and who did not think it prudent to molest us. It was bitterly cold, and we remained under arms till daybreak.

24th. We received confirmation that our camp had been menaced during the night, and that five hundred armed men had crossed the river, about two miles below us, on some hostile expedition. It is stated, also, that the Ameers intend marching out at the head of their army this night, and that their emissaries have been sent down the Indus to direct the boatmen in our employ to scuttle all the boats, and under penalty of death to quit our service. We sent again to Meer Noor Mahommed, demanding an answer to our message of yesterday, and informing him that we should positively depart at noon; in the meantime we despatched our treasure boats, containing five lakhs of rupees, under one half the guard, and having struck all our tents but one, embarked our baggage, and despatched it at 10 A. M., staying ourselves on shore till noon, with the steamer at the bank, in readiness to follow and protect our boats, in case any attempt should be made to follow them with the state barges which were moored a few hundred yards above us. At 8 A. M., the native agent, who had been sent the evening before with our message and letter to the Ameers, returned, stating that these princes had given him no answer until midnight, and that when he then attempted to make his way back to our camp, he was stopped by parties of Beloches whom he found watching round it. The answer given, was, that the treaty would be sent back, and that we might stay or go as we pleased, but that in the former case the Ameers would not answer for the conduct of their Beloches. At noon embarked and steamed down the Indus to Jerk, where we found that our boats had just arrived: we were four hours coming down, having grounded once, and been thereby detained three-quarters of an hour.

25th. The army arrived here, and it being determined to await the boats in the rear, an additional guard is sent down to meet them. At midnight, reports arrived that a strong body of Beloches had approached within four coss—in consequence of which the army turned out an hour before dawn, and remained under arms till daylight. At 10 A. M. I went with 50 of the Poona Auxiliary Horse to scour the jungle said to be occupied, but finding nobody there, we went on eleven miles, to the spot intended for our next ground, half way to Hyderabad; returning by a separate route, without seeing any appearance of the enemy.

27th. The Native Agent at Hyderabad writes that two of the Ameers, viz. Noor Mahommed and Nusser Khan, are still wavering, and inclined to yield, but that Meer Mahommed Khan and the Beloches are determined not to submit, and that Meer Shere Mahommed Khan of Meerpore with his army is on his way to join.—28th. The same Agent reports to-day, that a person is to be dispatched to our camp to-morrow, to propose a modification in the terms of the treaty.

29th. A deputation from the Ameers arrived, but merely delivered letters to the Commander-in-Chief and to the Resident, requesting an audience to-morrow, to communicate the messages which the letters stated they were deputed to deliver. Our spies from the Beloche camp at Hyderabad state, that this mission is only intended to delay our advance until the whole of their army, which is hourly increasing, shall have assembled.

30th. The deputation delivered their messages, which were expressive of the friendly intentions of the Ameers, but required explanations on certain points of the treaty, and solicited modifications in others, thus giving strength to the supposition that the object of the mission is of the nature represented above. Captain Carless, commanding the flotilla on the river, reports, that although within twelve miles of our camp, as the crow flies, he expects still to be three days in coming up. This day the bodies of three officers of the Queen's Royals, who had been missing since yesterday, were found. It appears that their distressing death had been caused by accident alone, although at first it was conjectured that they had been murdered, and that the jungle wherein their bodies were found had been set on fire to conceal the act. No trace whatever was to be discovered, however, of wounds, or external violence, and their bodies, being burned quite black, were scarcely recognizable. It is supposed that they must have become bewildered in the dense jungle of the neighbouring Shikargah, which has been on fire for the last two days, and thus were overtaken by the flames before they could extricate themselves.

31st. I took down between six and seven hundred camp followers to assist in tracking the boats; and got them all up to within a mile of camp by evening, the larger flat-bottomed vessel excepted, which was left half-way, although two hundred men were employed upon her. Went off the river into the Shikargah, which is still burning in some places, and fell in with the party sent to examine the spot where the bodies of the three officers were found. We picked up portions of their burned guns among the ash-heaps, which, together with other circumstances, satisfied us that their death had been entirely accidental. In the evening, accounts were brought from Hyderabad that Meer Shere Mahommed of Meerpore had arrived at that city with his army, and had plundered our grain depôts!

CHAPTER V.

SINDE—THE SUBMISSION OF THE AMEERS.

1st February. Boats were sent down to unload the large flat craft, by which means our stores will be all up to-morrow, and it is decided that we are to march the day after. Deputies from the Ameers arrived to intimate that their Highnesses had resolved to submit to the treaty, adding that the plunder of the granaries was in opposition to their authority, and that many persons had been killed in an attempt to prevent it. They further promised to repay the value of the grain, and requested a few verbal alterations in the treaty, with which their envoys returned to the capital. If the Ameers do ratify this treaty, which is not yet signed by them, they have probably resolved to do so as a mere temporary expedient, to get rid of us in consequence of their hearing that the Bengal Army is also marching down upon them. They know that our power at present is irresistible, but they hope when once in Affghanistan, we shall be so long and so fully occupied, that they may take measures to prevent our return through their country; expelling in the mean time the weak reserve we leave behind us; for it is difficult to believe that they have any intention of faithfully fulfilling the terms of the treaty.

2d. All the boats up.—3d. Marched eleven miles, to the ground to which I had patrolled on the 26th ultimo. Accounts from Hyderabad mention that the Ameers have ratified the treaty, returned into the fort from the camp they had occupied on the bank of the river, and ordered the dispersion of their army.

4th. To Kotree, fourteen miles, a village on the river opposite to the camp we left on the 24th ultimo. There is now no vestige left of the Beloche Army, which only the day before had occupied the opposite bank for two miles, to the amount of between sixteen and seventeen thousand men. We find that the Ameers have had the greatest difficulty in inducing the Beloches to withdraw, and that Shere Mahommed, having expressed his determination to oppose us was joined by the followers of all the other Ameers, when the latter returned into the fort the day before yesterday. Late last night, however, he had been prevailed on to retire, through the earnest and repeated entreaties of his friend Meer Sobdar Khan, (the prince who for his friendly disposition to us, has been favorably distinguished from the others in the new treaty) and by the distribution of upwards of five lakhs of rupees, as well as by its being represented to him that we had engaged not to cross the river, and would immediately pass on to Shirkarpore. The Ameers now express the utmost anxiety to fulfil the terms of the treaty, and immediately to make good Shah Soojah's tribute, together with the value of the grain lately plundered. This alacrity is caused by their having heard of the approach of the Bengal Army down the opposite side of the river, and of Shah Soojah's on this, not to mention a report that the latter has plundered Larkhana.—5th. A deputation arrived from Meer Sobdar Khan.—6th. Envoys also presented themselves from the Ameers, but no one from the camp has yet been allowed to cross the river to the city.

6th. The officers of our Army are permitted to visit the capital of Sinde under certain precautions to prevent disturbances. I accompanied the Chief Engineer, the Commandant and Brigade Major of Artillery with other scientific officers, and minutely inspected the city, fort, and environs of Hyderabad.

*   *   *   *
*   *   *   *
*   *   *   *
*   *   *   *
*   *   *   *

[The Journal from the 7th to the 18th of February has been lost. During that interval the author accompanied the Army to within a march of the Lukkee pass, where much difficulty was experienced in the passage of the Artillery. This pass is about eighty miles above Hyderabad, and six below the town of Sehwan. It may be turned by following the direct road from the latter place to Curachee, but cannot be avoided by following the right bank of the

Indus, as it abuts on the river. While these sheets are passing through the press it is reported that Government contemplate putting the Lukkee pass in a thorough state of repair.]

CHAPTER VI.

SEHWAN—THE ARRUL RIVER.

19th February. Went on to the Lukkee ghaut, seven miles, in anticipation of the arrival of his Excellency Sir Henry Fane, whose fleet is hourly expected: saw the last gun clear over the pass, which has been made practicable in an incredibly short time, through great skill on the part of the engineers, and extraordinary labour by the pioneers. No signs of Sir Henry Fane; staid at night in the Artillery camp at the top of the ghaut; the necessity of now making a passage over the ghaut is caused by the former road which wound round the base of the hill having been lately washed away by the Indus. That river now runs close under the termination of the Lukkee range, about a quarter of a mile below where the new road is constructed, which surmounts the ascent by a zigzag path, cut out of and built upon the almost perpendicular face of the hill.

20th. To Sehwan, six miles from the ghaut, a large and populous town situated on the Arrul river, about four miles above its junction with the Indus. Its stream is about two hundred feet broad, deep and muddy, but the current is sluggish, and a bridge of boats and pontoons which has been commenced over it is to be finished to-morrow. The remains of an ancient fortress at this place having been minutely described by other travellers, I shall not here enter upon the subject of the various conjectures as to its origin.* In the evening a note received from Sir Henry Fane, announced his arrival within a few miles, and his intention of continuing his voyage down to the junction of the two rivers in the evening.

21st. Accompanied Sir John Keane to the junction. After waiting some time Sir Henry Fane's fleet came in sight, and soon anchored, when the Generals met and embraced each other most cordially; breakfasted in Sir Henry's boat, and passed the day with him and his staff, each member of which had a separate boat comfortably fitted up. His Excellency being far from well was anxious to push on, and could not be persuaded to pass even a day in our camp, but rode thither in the evening, and held a durbar to receive a deputation sent by the Ameers to escort him to Hyderabad. He inspected our Ca-

* "The old castle of Sehwan, the erection of which is attributed to Alexander the Great, is perhaps the only veritable relict of the age of the Greeks, which can be traced in Sinde, and coins have been lately found in it, which, when submitted to the careful inspection of Mr. Prinsep, will probably attest its high antiquity, It is a mound of earth, nearly eighty feet in height, by fifteen hundred long, and eight hundred broad, intersected with subterraneous passages."—*Visit to Sinde, by J. Burnes, K. H.*

valry and Artillery horses on his way through the camp, and pronounced them good. This morning the Infantry and Cavalry brigades joined, but only a portion of their baggage had got clear of the Lukkee pass by nightfall.

22d. The Artillery passed over the pontoon bridge thrown across the Arrul river.—23d. Marched to Terooty, eight and a half miles; waited to see the Infantry and Cavalry pass the bridge, which operation occupied them an hour and a half. Encamped on the banks of an extensive lake, covered with wild duck and teeming with fish; route due north, over a well-cultivated country, covered, where devoid of cultivation, with coarse grass, the first almost that we had met with in Sinde. The Hala mountains branch off from the Lukkee range, and run parallel to our road about twenty miles distant. A Hurkarrah, (express messenger) five days from Shirkarpore, brings dispatches from Mr. Macnaghten, who presses our pushing on, and communicates a report that the Bolan pass is occupied by the enemy.

24th. Fourteen miles: by some mistake the Head-quarters' camp was pitched on the wrong road, and separated three miles from the army. The country passed over to-day was quite denuded of cultivation, and formed a strong contrast to yesterday's cheerful fertility, but every foot of it is cultivated at the proper season. Indeed this is the richest grain country perhaps in the world, yet we manage matters so badly that our camp followers are almost starving in consequence of the high prices:

pitched on the banks of the Indus.—25th. To Rookhun, eighteen miles, (three to the Army camp, and fifteen beyond) hard marching for our troops, who only leave their ground at day-break; pitched on the banks of the Indus, but two miles from its waters, a dry bed of that extent intervening.

26th. To Gulloo, ten miles, pitched on the banks of a little lake covered with duck: accompanied the Commander-in-Chief in a Native boat in search of game. A soldier robbed and wounded by a Native within a few yards of camp, in bright moonlight, and many of our camp followers have of late suffered in the same way.

27th. Fifteen miles, the country covered with alternate patches of the richest wheat fields and cypress jungle; pitched on the banks of the Indus. —28th. Seven miles, a pleasant march the whole way along the bank of the river, which we here take leave of, this being the last point of the Indus we touch on. At midday I was directed by Sir John Keane to proceed to Shirkarpore to communicate with Mr. Macnaghten, the envoy with Shah Soojah ool Moolk. Sent on two riding camels to the camp of the Auxiliary Horse, seven miles; followed in the evening, and, after a hasty meal with Colonel Cunningham, mounted one of the camels, and with the other carrying a few changes of clothes, pushed on to Larkhana, about twenty-six miles, only stopping to ferry the camels over the Maiee river, seven miles south of Larkhana, where, during the last day or two, it had risen so as to be no longer fordable—a circumstance which will cause much delay to our troops.

Reached Larkhana about 8 P. M., resting until 9 the following morning, and then started again on the same camels; rode all day and until 10 P. M. without any intermission; although latterly at a very slow pace in consequence of the excessive heat, and the fatigue of the camels. From Larkhana to Shirkarpore the distance has been measured fifty-two miles by the officers of the Shah's detachment, whilst marching between those places a few days since, when a rupture with the Hyderabad Ameers was expected. I found Mr. Macnaghten at table with his assistants, Major Todd and Captain McGregor, and was received with much cordiality by the Envoy, to whom I communicated the object of my journey.

I am indebted to the kindness of Captain James Holland, Deputy Quarter Master General, for the following information respecting the Arrul river and the lake mentioned in this chapter, which he has extracted from papers in his possession.

'From April to September, the period of the inundation, boatmen abandon the maiu stream of the Indus, and follow the course of the Arrul and Nara rivers from Sehwan to the junction of the latter stream near Sukhur.

The "Arrnl" seems to have been formed by the resistance offered to the current of the Indus by the Lukkee mountains, which, as before mentioned, abut on the river. A portion of the waters thus checked in their rapid course during the annual inundation, take an opposite (or northerly) direction to that of the main stream, for a distance of some twenty miles, where meeting a considerable extent of low ground, they expand into the "Munchur" Lake. This lake is, when full, about twenty miles in length from north to south, and perhaps half that breadth, with a considerable depth of water at all times in mid channel. From its northern extremity, the Nara river pursues a winding course of about one hundred and fifty miles (nearly double its direct distance) to the Indus, which it joins, as before stated, some miles below Sukhur.

The course of the Arrul is remarkably straight, that of the Nara as remarkably crooked, its name, signifying a snake, has been appropriately given in consequence. The greater part of the course of the Nara passes through an exceedingly rich soil, in which rice and cotton are the principal subjects of cultivation. The Munchur Lake is covered with the Lotus plant, and abounds in fish. Numerous families live in their boats on its surface, and gain a subsistence from the produce of their nets.'

CHAPTER VII.

SHAH SHOOJA OOL MOOLK—UPPER SINDE.

2d March. All the officers of the Bengal Commissariat department were assembled in Mr. Macnaghten's tent, to afford me the information required by Sir John Keane. Wrote to His Excellency to inform him of the result, which was much more favorable in some respects than he had expected. An audience with Shah Shooja ool Moolk was appointed for the afternoon; but, when the time arrived, His Majesty was so overcome by the heat, (104° in the shade,) that he sent to beg we would join him in his evening promenade. We went accordingly, accompanied by Major Todd, and found the king sitting in a tukht-i-ruwan, or native litter: conversed with His Majesty for a few minutes, during which we remained on horseback. It is customary to approach and leave the Shah with much ceremony, and this etiquette is scrupulously observed by the British Officers. His Majesty was very affable : he appears between fifty and sixty years of age, and of mild manners.

3d. Sunday. Walked through the lines of Shah Shooja's recently-raised army, which is better equipped than I had expected to find it; but no opportunity having yet presented itself of seeing the levy out, I could not form an opinion of the state of its discipline. Despatches have been received from Sir Willoughby Cotton, who is advancing to the Bolan pass with the Bengal column, and also from Lieutenant Pottinger. The latter writes from Herat, and gives a very satisfactory account of the power and influence he still maintains, but the greatest distress is represented to prevail there from scarcity. The intended return of the Persian army was reported, but nothing certain is known as to whether it was really approaching or not. Sir Willoughby Cotton gives a most deplorable account of the scarcity of water and forage on this route, which is so great, that only one squadron of Cavalry, or one wing of Infantry, can advance at a time: many days will consequently be occupied in the passage of his troops. His Artillery Park and the 2d Infantry Brigade had not yet left Shikarpore, nor were they likely to do so in less than a week. The Shah, with his army, and the mission, purposed marching on the 7th, but it is now doubtful whether they can advance so soon, in consequence of this obstruction of the Bengal column. Having previously sent off my riding camels half way to Larkhana, I took leave of Mr. Macnaghten after dinner, and departed at midnight in a palankeen for the half-way station, where I arrived at 7 A. M.

4th. Mounted the camels and arrived at half-past 11 A. M. at Larkhana, where I found the army had just encamped. The country between Larkhana and Shikarpore is more thickly covered with jungle, consisting chiefly of stunted baubul, than any I had yet seen in Sinde. Wrote to Mr. Macnaghten thanking him for an offer, conveyed through Sir John Keane, which had passed me on the road, to attach me to his mission, but respectfully declining the favor, as I am unwilling to leave the army whilst a prospect of service remains. The report of the Bolan pass being occupied by the enemy proves to be unfounded, the Khelat chief, in whose territory it is situated, having been secured to our interests; but such difficulties are encountered by Sir Willoughby Cotton's column, owing to scarcity of water and forage, that it is hardly possible we can follow by the same route; the forage at any rate being all consumed. The practicability of entering Candahar via Khelat, is therefore under discussion, by ascending the Moolan pass from Gundava, to inspect which route officers will proceed to-morrow.

5th. Despatches from Sir Willoughby Cotton represent his difficulties to be increasing, his hopes of a supply of water by cutting through certain embankments in the upper country having proved futile, from the circumstance of the water thus obtained being absorbed by the parched tract intervening. His column is, however, creeping on slowly, by small detachments. The march of the Bombay Army is delayed from a deficiency of camels, half of those brought up with us being now disabled or lost, whilst the stores hitherto transported by water now require land carriage. Notwithstanding all the assistance derived from the Bengal Army, it is quite evident, that the whole of our division cannot possibly proceed; and the Commander-in-Chief has with great regret accordingly been compelled to leave behind, until further carriage can be provided, the three regiments of Bengal Native Infantry, which are still at Shikarpore, and also three Bombay Native regiments,—the latter in reserve at Sukkur on the Indus, opposite to the fort of Bukkur,*—where the Bombay Grenadiers will remain in garrison. It is doubtful how far we shall be able to carry on even the remainder with a suitable commissariat.

6th. To add to Sir Willoughby Cotton's difficulties he now reports that his cavalry baggage has been attacked by plunderers.—7th. The Shah, with half his army, (the remainder being left at Shikarpore for want of carriage,) and accompanied by Mr. Macnaghten, marched from that place with the intention

* The fortress of Bukkur covers an insulated rock in a bend of the river Indus, having the towns of Sukkur and Roree immediately opposite on the right and left banks. The fort is about seven hundred yards in length, by three hundred in extreme breadth. The breadth of the divided stream, immediately between the island and the towns named, is only one hundred and seventy and eighty yards, but at the southern extremity, where the bridges of boats were laid down for the passage of the Bengal Army, they are about three hundred and fifty and one hundred and ten yards respectively. The waters rush with great rapidity through these narrow channels, especially during the inundation, and accidents frequently happen to boats from their violence.

Note by Captain James Holland, Dy. Qr. Mr. Genl.

of pursuing a route parallel to, but westward of, that taken by Sir Willoughby Cotton. The commencement of his march, however, has proved very unpropitious, two hundred and fifty of his camels having disappeared during the first day. Our Cutch camelmen having struck work since our arrival here, and, in spite of every persuasion, positively refused to advance, I was deputed to quell the mutiny, and accordingly assembled them all, to the number of two or three thousand, when, having selected twenty of the most influential of their jemadars, I marched them off in confinement, each under a separate guard. I then ordered the remainder to take out their camels, under the surveillance of a body of horse, but they refused. Having warned them, without effect, that we could be trifled with no longer, and of my determination to flog them all round unless they complied, I was under the necessity of tying up one and giving him two dozen lashes: a second succeeded, and a third,—who got four dozen, he having been observed checking the rest when they began to show symptoms of giving in. This had the desired effect; they promised obedience in future, and took out the camels to graze. On their return in the evening, they were again mustered, and told that they should remain under surveillance, unless such of the Cutch jemadars as had been faithful throughout should pledge themselves for their good conduct: the required pledge having been given, they were sent to their duty. The jemadars in confinement will, however, remain so for the present, as a further security.

8th. The lately refractory camel-men quite obedient to-day. The Grenadier regiment of Bombay Native Infantry marched to occupy the fort of Bukkur.—9th. The last few days have been exceedingly hot, and, to-day, the thermometer stands at 105° in the tents.—10th. A change in the weather, which has become quite cold in the morning, and much cooler during the day than it was. Arrangements having been completed for our advance, the army is ordered to march by three detachments, the first proceeding to-morrow, and the others on the following successive days; but we are doubtful whether the scarcity of water will admit even of these small bodies proceeding without further subdivision. —11th. The first detachment, H. M. 17th and 2d Regiments of Foot, marched. The Commander-in-Chief and Staff will follow to-morrow.

12th. Sir John Keane and Staff marched with a detachment, consisting of Horse Artillery, 1st Bombay Cavalry, and a wing of the 19th Regiment Bombay N. I. to Kumbar, fifteen miles: until within three miles of the halting ground, the road generally threaded the channel of a dry canal, except in a few places, where the sand was so heavy as to oblige us to ascend the sides, which are not less than thirty feet high, and mostly very steep: the average width of this canal is about sixty feet, and along both sides there are innumerable wells, from which the water is raised by means of the Persian wheel. There are several small villages on either bank, and many visible also in the distance, but the intermediate country is chiefly covered with low tamarisk jungle.

A flat-bottomed boat, about thirty feet in length, was lying in the dry bed of the canal, about the middle of our march—a proof that, when filled, it is navigable for this description of craft. A new feature in the landscape at Larkhana, and around every village on this march, presented itself, in the numerous date trees, which had not heretofore in any numbers appeared in our route through Sinde. The natives of this country have not acquired the art of tapping the date tree, nor does it appear to be of use in any way, the fruit never coming to maturity.

13th. Ten miles, over a level plain, as smooth as a bowling-green, with scarcely any villages or cultivation, but occasionally exhibiting clumps of stunted tamarisk. Last night, about twenty of the Government camels were carried off by men hired to take care of them. We passed eight or ten dead camels, which had been left by the Brigade that had preceded us; several of our own also died of a contagious disease, which appears to have broken out amongst them.

14th. A march of fourteen miles. Stayed in the rear, to ascertain whether any more camels had been taken off during the night, and was glad to find that the precautions adopted since yesterday had proved effectual—no further desertion having taken place. The villages on this route, together with that at our encamping ground, have been deserted for the last two months, from a dread of the Khelat Beloches, who have ravaged this frontier since it was left unprotected by the Sindian Garrisons stationed for their protection, but who were summoned to Hyderabad when opposition to us was contemplated, and have not yet returned. The wells are few in number, and from not having been lately drawn, the water is at first very bad, though it improves as it is taken out. Great difficulty is experienced in watering so many horses and camels; but we are, nevertheless, obliged to halt here, in order to refresh the latter, previously to crossing a desert of thirty miles in extent, which now lies before us. Curbee in abundance is found at all the deserted villages in the neighbourhood. By some accident the village unfortunately took fire, and, being surrounded and filled with combustible matter, it was found impossible to subdue the flames, which blazed the whole night. Being totally without inhabitants, nothing of any value could have been destroyed, but the affair will, doubtless, be magnified by the tongue of report, and our credit in the country will suffer accordingly.

CHAPTER VIII.

UPPER SINDE—CUTCH GUNDAVA.

15th. Messed early, and sent off our baggage at 5 P. M., starting ourselves at the same time, and marching at a rapid pace till half-past 8 in the evening. Bivouacked till half-past 2, then mounted again, and arrived at Chikul, on the opposite side of the desert, at about half-past 7 in the morning, the total distance being above thirty miles. The three or four first and last miles, before entering and after leaving the desert, were over a very heavy sandy road, the intermediate space being a hard, smooth surface, totally devoid of bushes or vegetation of any sort. Our road extended almost due west as far as the ground chosen for encampment, which was within three or four miles of the Hala mountains, here considerably higher than the Lukkee range. The village is of some extent, but totally deserted, either in consequence of our arrival, or from a dread of the Sindians on the other side of the desert. In its neighbourhood is a plentiful supply of water in small running streams, intersecting beautiful fields of standing corn. The brother of the Chief of this district, which is under Khelat, waited on Major Todd to tender his services, which were made use of, to induce the inhabitants to return to their villages. At 8 P. M. I departed *dak*, on a mission to Shah Shooja ool Moolk, or rather to the Envoy and Minister, from whose camp the more recent accounts have been anything but cheering. They represent the troops in advance to be greatly crippled for want of carriage, and the country to have suffered much from the rapacity of the Shah's levies.

17th. Travelled all night, and at dawn of day arrived at Jull, nineteen miles, where I left behind me six Poona horsemen who had formed my escort, and mounted a camel which I had sent on a previous day; but the poor animal having crossed the desert only just before, and travelled also the greater part of last night, was already much fatigued. Arrived at Gundava, twenty-two miles, about 10 A. M., and waited there till 1 o'clock for Lieutenant Threshie of the Commissariat, who, on his arrival, lent me a pony to carry me to Baugh, as an escort to which place I entertained two armed Beloches. Travelled at an ambling pace from 1 till 8 P. M. to Gool Mahommed ke Got, where I found a detachment of the Shah's Army which had missed the direct road, and learning from them that the Envoy was expected to arrive at Baugh the following morning, I bivouacked for the night. I estimated that I had travelled about five-and-thirty miles from Gundava, the road leading over the usual flat sterile country, on which there are traces of fields that have not been cultivated for some seasons, in consequence, apparently, of the scarcity of water. A strong evidence of the lawless state of society in this country is observable in the numerous small watch-towers, about twenty feet in height, which are scattered over the whole plain that I traversed to-day, serving as places of refuge for the peasantry, when attacked, from which they can defend their persons and property.

18th. Continued my journey to Baugh, 10 miles; found the Shah's camp pitched, but the Envoy's suite having missed the road, were still behind. I therefore accompanied Mr. Macnaghten and his assistants to the tent of Lieutenant Conolly, who, being on duty with the Shah's escort, had come on the day before. Here, after having breakfasted, I passed the day with the Envoy.

19th. Rode out with Mr. Macnaghten to inspect some fields, said to have been plundered by the Shah's troops, and found the tale too true, a very considerable extent of cultivation having been completely swept away. The Envoy has often had occasion to remonstrate with the Shah on this subject, and is now resolved to adopt more energetic measures to check an evil, which, besides being injurious to the people of the country, and to the troops that have to follow in the track of the King's levy, must increase the difficulty of restraining the followers of our own armies from similar plunder. I was sorry to learn that the baggage of the Shah's Army has been exposed on its march, and latterly more especially, to the extensive depredation of hordes of Beloches, and that many murders have also been committed. In a country, however, where every strong man's hand is raised against his weaker neighbour, such occurrences could hardly be prevented, even by the most determined measures and by the severest examples.

Having fulfilled the objects of my mission, I departed at 11 A. M., and at 8 P. M. arrived at Gundava, where I halted for the night, on hearing that our army was to arrive the next morning at Punjook, about ten miles distant. In consequence of information received that four mounted Beloche banditti were on the road before me, I was kept on the alert during the whole of the latter part of this march, my Beloche guides carrying their matchlocks lighted. We were not, however, molested by any one.

20th March. Met the Commander-in-Chief at Punjook, 10 miles. In consequence of my communications, it is determined that I shall return to Gundava this evening, for the purpose of despatching thence an express messenger to Mr. Macnaghten. His Excellency has now decided upon pushing on with a small escort to Dadur, there to meet the Shah, and accompany him and the Envoy up the Bolan Pass, which is now occupied by our troops. The last accounts from Sir Willoughby Cotton, received while I was at Baugh, represented that the head of his column was then within one march of the top of the Pass, and although the Candahar chiefs were said to have moved out with the intention of opposing him there, it was now quite impossible they could arrive in time. It was supposed, therefore, that they would return to Candahar, where it is said they are making preparations to resist us, one of them having, it is reported, assumed the dignity of "Leader of the Faithful," to give a religious colour to their cause ; Mahommedans considering it martyrdom to die in the field, under an appointed prince of the faith. It is believed, however, that dissensions are already rife amongst the brothers, and Mr. Macnaghten considers that everything will be arranged through the agency of diplomacy, backed by gold. On my return to Gundava in the evening, I heard of many mounted robbers lurking in the neighbourhood of our camp, which is now beginning to be harassed by plunderers in the same manner as the Bengal Army and the Shah's troops have been for some time past.

21st. In riding out to meet the Commander-in-Chief this morning, I met with an unfortunate accident, which is likely to confine me to my couch for some time : my horse, in making a sudden turn when at speed, fell flat on his side, with me below him, the result being that the bone of the pelvis, above the hip joint, was fractured, in consequence of coming into violent contact with the hilt of my sword. No other inconvenience to me than delay, will probably result from this, but it is excessively vexatious to be confined at such a juncture. The medical officers assure me, however, that three weeks are the utmost of detention that I shall suffer, and that although I cannot accompany Sir John Keane in advance, I can be carried in a palankeen with the troops that are to follow a few days hence.

22d. Preparations are being made for Sir John Keane's departure, and Major General Willshire is in general orders to command the "Bombay division of the Army of the Indus."—23d. The Commander-in-Chief departed, accompanied by his personal Staff; his escort being a wing of the First Light Cavalry, and half of the 19th Regiment Native Infantry. His Excellency purposes marching by the route which skirts the hills, and expects to arrive at Dadur on the 27th instant.

24th. Accounts have been received that the kafila of camels, now *en route* from Shirkapore, and on which the advance of the Bombay division chiefly depends, has been detained in consequence of the canals between this and Kunda being flooded. Our only dependance now, is on some Camels expected to be sent back from Dadur. The days are becoming exceedingly hot; and the thermometer has risen to 104° in the shade.

26th. Accounts from Mr. Macnaghten's camp mention, that some of the advance baggage of the Shah's Army had been attacked by Beloche robbers, in a pass between Baugh and Dadur. The audacity of the marauders in the Shah's neighbourhood appears to be increasing, but in our vicinity we hear little of them at present, and a sharp look out having been kept, we have recovered most of what we had previously lost since crossing the desert. I am now so far recovered as to admit of my being moved sufficiently to change my inner garments for the first time since my accident. In fact, I am recovering so fast, that the surgeons say I may be carried forward to-morrow, should an order to advance be issued.

27th. I am able to-day to bear raising in bed sufficiently to permit me to write. A report has been received from Captain Stockley, who was proceeding in charge of a convoy of camels from Shirkarpore to Dadur, that he is beleaguered by Beloche plunderers hovering around him, and carrying off his camels while on the line of march, in open day, and in the teeth of an escort of Bengal regular Infantry. He has been obliged in consequence to take refuge in a deserted fort, two marches from Shirkapore, until reinforcements of cavalry shall be sent out to him, having already lost between two and three hundred camels. Those coming from Dadur and Baugh, for which our force is halted, are now arriving in detachments.

28th. Letters from the Commander-in-Chief mention his having met the Shah and the Envoy on the 26th instant, within a short march of Dadur, whither they were to proceed together the next day, and there to halt for a day or two prior to entering the pass. There are accounts of Sir Willoughby Cotton's column having surmounted the pass. The Commander-in-Chief's camp is suffering from the depredations of Beloches, two of whom taken in the act of plundering were hanged on the 26th instant. Every thing is now prepared for our advance, and the Artillery Brigade is to march to-morrow, the Infantry following it the next day.

30th. The Infantry and Dragoons, who were to have marched to-day, are delayed until to-morrow, in consequence of certain Commissariat arrangements being still incomplete.—31st. To Gurgur, six-and-a-half miles, in a due westerly direction, to the foot of the hills, where we encamped on the banks of some small running streams, which supply water to the fields through artificial channels. I did not feel the slightest inconvenience from the shaking in the palankeen; and, in fact, were it not necessary to remain quiet, in order to allow the fractured bone to unite, I believe I might now walk about.

CHAPTER IX.

CUTCH GUNDAVA—DADUR.

April 1st. Advanced on Shoorun, fourteen miles due North, along the foot of the mountains, and encamped one-and-a-half miles beyond, to shorten tomorrow's march, which will still be upwards of twenty miles, there being no intermediate water. I this day completed twenty years of uninterrupted service in India.

2d. Marched at midnight, by the moon's light, to Sooner, twenty-two miles, across a perfect desert, the first part being generally over heavy sand, and the last five or six miles covered with large stones and pebbles, appearing to have been washed down from the hills, on which traces of water channels are everywhere perceptible. Passed the bodies of two Beloche robbers on the road, said to have fallen yesterday in a skirmish with the people belonging to Ahmed Khan, a person of some authority in this country, who is accompanying the Brigade in advance. Accounts received from it mention an affair also with robbers on the line of march yesterday, in which a Sepoy of the 19th Regt. was wounded, who is since dead. This, however, occurred within two miles of camp, and the bodies we saw were eight miles from it.

A Havildar and five Sepoys of the 19th Regiment N. I. succeeded in repulsing a large body of Beloches, who attempted to carry off two camels, of which the former were in charge, but the robbers were more successful the previous day, having seized some camels which were escorted by two of the Horse Artillery recruits, who escaped slightly wounded, although they do not appear to have used their own arms, or to have resisted the attack. The party of the 19th N. I. is supposed to have killed two and wounded a third, all of whom were carried off by their comrades. Accounts from the advance represent the daily increasing audacity of the Beloches, notwithstanding that many have been shot in their attempts made on the baggage, and two others hanged. They have been too frequently successful in their object to be readily deterred, and have killed numbers of our followers; each day's accounts mentioning several casualties both among the Shah's troops and the Bengal corps. Here are plenty of running streams and green crops in abundance, but no supplies whatever.

3d. A halt. In the course of yesterday, information was brought to us that some stragglers had been attacked. A detachment of horse was sent out, which overtook a small party of the robbers, who were leading off two of our camels. On seeing the horsemen they threw away their arms, and attempted to conceal themselves in holes and bushes; but four were slain, and the others made prisoners. The stragglers proved to be three Europeans, who, having gone off the line of march to sleep, were surprised, one of them being killed, the second wounded, and left for dead, whilst the third effected his escape. It is believed that in the course of the day above twenty camels with much other plunder fell to the banditti hovering along the line of march and about the camp, where they continued their attempts during the whole night. The Dragoon sentries being on the alert, cut down a camp follower, who, when challenged, attempted to sneak off instead of replying. Accounts, from the Artillery Brigade in advance, state, that, on the route we are to follow to-night, their baggage was repeatedly attacked by large bands of robbers, six of whom had been killed without any loss on the side of the British, save one man and two horses slightly wounded. The last three days have been very hot, the thermometer ranging from 104° to 108° in the shade. A violent storm of wind and dust blew during the night, accompanied by a few drops of rain: one camel-man was wounded to-day, but no other damage was ascertained to have been done by the Beloches.

4th. Marched at midnight to Noushara, eighteen miles. The baggage having been kept together and strongly guarded, no molestation was offered to it during this march, although the road for the first few miles was particularly favourable for ambush and attack,—being bounded by small hills and jungle, and crossed occasionally by deep ravines. It is presumed that the reception the Beloches met with from the preceding Brigade must have taught them caution. We found the rear-guard of the Artillery still on the ground when we arrived, and learned that they had been on the alert all the preceding day, and under arms all night, in consequence of the reports of large assemblages of Beloches in this neighbourhood. Some attempts had been made on the camels yesterday, but with what result we have not yet learned. We understand, however, that more of the marauders were slain, and that about twenty stolen camels were recovered from them in the pursuit.

A striking proof of the audacity of these banditti was given shortly after breakfast this morning, when three of them came on horseback to the very skirts of the camp, and, having stripped two camel-men of their property, drove off six camels. The cries of the sufferers being heard at the tents, some troopers instantly mounted, and, giving chase, rescued the camels, and brought in the head of one of the plunderers. Several other Beloches being observed skulking in a jungle that skirted the river about a mile distant, a party of the Cavalry was sent out, which succeeded in killing thirteen of them, besides making four prisoners. At a deep ravine that crosses the road, about five miles from the last camp, our rear-guard, consisting of a detachment of H. M. 17th, and Queen's Royal Regiment, was reconnoitred by a body of fifty or sixty Beloches; but a volley dispersed them, although with what loss is not known. No casualties occurred amongst our own people in the affair to-day.

5th. To Dadur, seven-and-a-half miles; nothing

seen of the Beloches. This day joined the Artillery
Brigade and some detachments of Bengal Infantry.
The latter, which had been here since the Bengal
Army advanced, report, that the aggressions of the
Beloches had been, up to yesterday, constant and
daring, and rewarded occasionally with booty, although many of the plunderers had been slain.
Numerous individuals belonging to the Army had
also fallen, but wherever a determined stand had
been made, however great the disproportion of the
parties, the robbers had been invariably beaten off.
No accounts have been received from Sir John Keane,
or from the Envoy, since they entered the pass on the
29th ultimo; and for many days past we have received
no post whatever from Shikarpore. Open communication with front and rear is, in fact, entirely cut
off, except by large detachments, which are invariably either attacked or menaced by strong bodies
of Beloche horse: even Cossids in disguise have
rarely contrived to elude the vigilance of the banditti, who are ever on the watch around us. The
35th Bengal Regiment of Native Infantry, which
passed up three days ago, is reported to have had a
smart brush in the pass, but the particulars are not
ascertained. We are obliged to wait here for the
convoy of provisions coming from Shikarpore under
Captain Stockley, whom losses, from repeated attacks
by Beloches, drove to seek refuge, on the 2d ultimo,
in a fort, two marches on this side of Shikàrpore,
since which date no tidings have been received of
him.

6th. Dispatches from Captain Stockley announce

his arrival yesterday at Bony, three marches hence. He intended halting there to-day, and arriving here on the 9th instant. It appears that Captain Stockley was reinforced on the 20th instant by Brigadier Dennie, in person, with the wing of a regiment, and some horse, since which date, although frequently menaced by large bodies of horse, no attempt had been made upon the convoy. In occasional skirmishing, one or two had been killed on each side; and two of the prisoners taken had avowed themselves the servants of an influential chief residing not far from Baugh, who has directed his followers to do their utmost to injure the supporters of the Shah,—the Beloches being resolved, they say, never to submit to him. This avowal, together with the systematic, determined, and continued aggressions of armed bodies along our whole line of march, for so many days past, makes it very apparent that our tormentors are instigated by something beyond mere individual plunder; and there can be little doubt that Dost Mahommed Khan, with the Candahar chiefs, must be exercising an influence over the chieftains of this country, stronger than that established by our gold. Native report states, that the quiet enjoyed by us, for the last two days, is caused by Beloches having assembled in the hills, with the intention of opposing us in the pass. This is the best policy that could be adopted by the Affghans: had they faced us in force, they must have been conquered, with great *éclat* to Shah Shooja's cause, which would thus at once have been established; but by permitting the main army to surmount the pass unmolested, and then letting loose swarms of marauders on our rear, to cut off our supplies, while, at the same time, they destroy everything in our front, they take the only possible mode of opposing us with success. Whether they have adopted this plan or not, we have no means of ascertaining, being altogether ignorant of what is transpiring in advance; but occurrences in the rear savour strongly of an organized system of opposition. It is decided that our first detachment, consisting of Artillery (both horse and foot), with H. M.'s 17th Foot, shall advance to the pass on the 9th instant, and the remainder of the Bombay Division on the 12th.

7th. In the evening, a band of marauders carried off several camels, which were grazing near the camp; and, having been pursued by a party of cavalry, three were killed, and one taken prisoner— the camels being all rescued, and one cavalry horse only wounded in the affair. An officer's horse was, last night, twice carried off from his picquet, in the midst of camp. Separate dawks arrived from the advance army to-day, from which we learn that the pass is unoccupied.

CHAPTER X.

THE BOLAN PASS.

8th April. Our spies from the Bolan pass report that the tribes which occupied it, having quarrelled and fought among themselves about the division of booty, no opponents are now to be seen.—9th. Marched with the Artillery Brigade, escorted by H. M.'s 17th Foot, eleven-and-a-half miles into the pass, along the bed of the Bolan river, the channel of which is the only road; a stream of clear water, from thirty to forty feet broad, and from one to three in depth, crossing the road six times. During the floods, the stream, which is in some places confined between perpendicular precipices, within a channel sixty or eighty feet wide, would preclude the possibility of escape to an army caught in the torrent. The mountains on every side are the most abrupt, sterile, and inhospitable, I ever beheld—not a blade of vegetation of any kind being found, save in the bed of the stream, where there is some coarse grass, on which horses and camels pick a scanty subsistence. The mountains are as repulsive in appearance as they are barren in reality, being everywhere of a dull and uniform brown colour.

The scarcity of forage throughout the pass, which extends to seven marches, renders it indispensable that we should take with us grain for the camels, and as much grass or straw as can be carried. All the detachments which have preceded us have suffered lamentably, owing to a neglect of precaution in this respect; a fact which is attested by the putrifying carcases of camels, which are scattered along the whole route. Beloche scouts were occasionally seen on the heights, flanking our road; but, warned by the disasters of our predecessors, such precautions had been adopted, to guard our baggage, that the banditti found no opportunity of pouncing upon it. Distressing evidence presented itself of their previous handywork, in the bodies of upwards of thirty Sepoys and followers of the Bengal and Shah's columns, which were lying exposed on the road, together with the remains of carts, by burning which, others of the slain appeared to have been consumed. In the evening, information was brought that the Beloches were assembled in our neighbourhood, to the number of about three thousand, and were preparing for an attack, either at night, or on the line of march tomorrow morning. Had they come, we were well prepared to receive them; but our slumbers were undisturbed, except by a single shot, fired by a sentry, either at a real or supposed enemy lurking in our front.

Accounts from the Envoy's camp, dated the 6th, place our prospects in advance in a very gloomy light, as regards the supplies to be expected; the combined troops of the Shah and of the Bengal column having been obliged to push on to Pisheen, with only ten days' half-rations per man, and none for the cattle; coupled with the assurance of a very limited supply in that valley; there being, moreover, nothing whatever on the other side, until they shall arrive at Candahar, which is thirteen marches beyond. This deficiency is caused by the non-redemption, by the Khan of Khelat, of his pledge to lay in supplies for us at Shawl. Sir Alexander Burnes had proceeded to Khelat, to bring the Khan to the camp, and obtain his co-operation and assistance; but little advantage is expected to accrue from the measure, and our Division, having to follow in the steps of other armies, will, it is feared, find the country totally exhausted. We are provided, however, with about twenty days' provisions for the troops, and rations for the horses, as far as the top of the pass, where it is hoped forage will be found sufficient to subsist them. Unfortunately, little assistance can be expected from the rear; for if any convoys are on their way from Shikarpore (which is uncertain), they cannot overtake us before our present stock is exhausted.

10th. Marched at day-break, the first mile through a narrow defile with precipitous scarps, three or four hundred feet high on either side. Beloche scouts were seen by the advanced guard, but they did not show in strength until the rear guard left the ground, when they appeared in great numbers on the heights, and about fifty having ventured down into the plain, were charged by the horse attached to the rear guard, who cut down five of them, suffering no loss themselves, although exposed to a heavy fire opened by the Beloches posted on the ridges, in order to cover the flight of their comrades. After this affair our column was menaced no longer. It is clear that the marauders had watched the whole line of baggage, in the hope of finding some portion exposed, on which they might pounce with impunity; until, at last, the arrival of the rear guard rendering this no longer probable, they immediately showed themselves. This day's march was about thirteen-and-a-half miles, and very similar to that of yesterday; the road crossing the stream no less than seventeen times.

11th. Left the river and marched nine miles through a broad valley covered with loose pebbles and large stones, and evidently overflowed at some seasons, although at present there is not a drop of water, except in a shallow stream at our encamping ground.—12th. Advanced ten miles, across a second valley, of the same description as that crossed yesterday, affording no water save at the encamping ground.—13th. A march of eight miles: road much the same as before, covered with loose stones, most trying to cattle and guns. Numbers of our camels have sunk during the last two marches, owing to the ruggedness of the road, and the paucity of food. Passed several bodies of murdered followers of former detachments, lying a little off the road. Running water was met with occasionally during the march, a delicious stream gushing from the side of a hill at our encamping ground. The hills now appear to differ slightly in character from those hitherto passed, and are here and there clothed with scanty vegetation.

14th. Marched at half-past 1 P. M., the first six or seven miles through a narrow defile, seldom more than sixty or seventy yards in width, and commanded by perpendicular scarps on both sides, from one to three hundred feet high; the road, as before, being over loose shingle, which proved most fatiguing both to man and horse. In the next three or four miles the valley widens, and the stones cease, while the hills on either side become less precipitous, and now and then a few stunted trees and bushes appearing, form an agreeable relief to the eye, accustomed for so many days past to the most dismal sterility. About ten miles from our last ground, occurs a steep and heavy ascent, of above one hundred yards, which was surmounted by all the guns without accident, although not without considerable labour. At 9 P. M., we bivouacked about five miles beyond the ghaut, from which the descent is gradual to Shawl. The valley, widening as we advanced, presented a surface totally devoid of stones, and covered with southern wood, which the camels devoured greedily.

With the ascent last mentioned terminates the Bolan Pass, of which we are now clear. The rise up to that point, although almost imperceptible, and probably not exceeding one foot in a hundred, would yield a considerable height, the pass being about seventy-five miles in length. The alteration in the climate has been very decided and agreeable; there being a difference of not less than twenty degrees in the temperature since we left Dadur. Many of the Kakurs, (a wild tribe, occupying the upper part of the pass), were seen this evening on the heights on both sides of the defile. Being apparently unarmed, and not offering to molest us, we took no notice of them. They were probably looking out for abandoned camels; but the bodies of several persons on the road, stragglers of the preceding columns, shewed that they can commit murder also when the defenceless fall into their power. In the narrow defile, the stench arising from the countless putrifying camels, was dreadful. The fact of there being no water within twenty-eight miles, dictated this evening's march, and we bivouacked on the ground about five miles to the westward of the ghaut.

15th. Marched about 3 A. M., and, arriving in five hours within sight of Seeree, encamped about two miles short of that place. Seeree is a considerable village, and the first we had seen since entering the pass. The country now wears a more favorable aspect, the valleys widening and gradually descending towards Shawl; whilst the northern face of some high hills to our left, display patches of snow, of which I had seen none for twenty long years. Passed on the road side the body of a recently-murdered Cossid, who doubtless had charge of letters for us. These messengers, now our only means of communication, usually travel here, as in all eastern countries, in perfect safety, respected as religious mendicants, but few have lately reached their destination; and, as hardly a single letter has been received from the advance for the last fortnight, it is most probable that those dispatched by us have shared a similar fate. Several dead bodies lie exposed in the neighbourhood, supposed to be those of camp followers of the preceding detachments. All stores and baggage were brought up in the course of the day except some of the park waggons, for which the rear guard is detained, and which cannot arrive until to-morrow. Food and water were sent to them. Large bodies of marauders hovered along the line of march up to the pass, but only succeeded in plundering two or three stragglers, and those without having recourse to murder. Some shots were exchanged between them and the rear-guard with no apparent effect.

16th. Went on to Quetta, ten miles, where Major Todd had preceded me the evening before. A brigade of Bengal and Shah's troops are stationed here, and an officer is placed in political charge of the district, which, being an appanage of Khelat, would denote that the conduct of that Chief is about to meet its reward. Notwithstanding his offers to meet the Shah, vows of allegiance, promise of assistance to us, and the treaty he has just concluded with Sir Alexander Burnes, he has not waited upon the Shah; but, being in close communication with Dost Mahommed Khan, has not only withheld the promised assistance, but has allowed his people to plunder the bearers of the treaty, and even to carry off that document! The Bengal and Shah's Armies were detained at the fourth march from this place by a ghaut which required clearing, and they did not commence their passage over it until the 13th instant. From this point it is six marches to Candahar. Some little improvement had taken place in the state of the supplies of the force, a little grain and some camels having been procured on the march: but they, as well as ourselves, are on half rations, and the little flour to be obtained is selling at two and three seers the rupee. A convoy of provisions from the rear, comprising about one week's supply, passed us yesterday, to overtake the advance.

CHAPTER XI.

AFFGHANISTAN—CANDAHAR.

17th April. Quetta.—The Artillery Brigade came up. The mules of the 19-pr. battery being completely exhausted, arrangements have been made for leaving it behind, and pushing on with the other, and with the Horse Artillery. No direct accounts from the advance; and the native reports are most contradictory as to the intentions or preparations of the Candahar Chiefs to oppose us. Some officers, visiting the gardens surrounding this town, were most agreeably surprised to find a great variety of English shrubs and fruit-trees, some in full blossom, and others in young fruit. Peaches, apricots, plums, grapes and apples, sweet-briar, hawthorn, Mayflower, many beautiful specimens of which last, in luxuriant blossom, were brought to me, together with various kinds of roses, one of which, of an orange and yellow colour, is singular in yielding a most disagreeable odour. The fields and plains in this valley likewise display many flowers familiar to us, such as the crocus, butter-cup, corn-flower, lily, poppy, and dandelion.

18th. Our preparations being still incomplete, we are unable to march. General Willshire has arrived with the rear Brigade at Seeree, our last march. His baggage was attacked with considerable spirit at the pass, and whilst forty-nine camel-loads of grain were carried off, five horses killed, and three troopers wounded, on our side, many of the enemy are said to have been killed.

19th. Marched at day-break to Cutch Lack, nine miles, descending a steep ghaut about half-way, where the baggage of the previous divisions had been attacked with greater spirit than had been heretofore displayed. We expected a skirmish, but although many armed men were observed on the heights, they did not venture within shot until the rear-guard came up, when they approached nearer, and a few long shots were exchanged to no apparent purpose. Three dead bodies, exposed at the top of the pass, are supposed to be those of our missing Cossids.

20th. To Hyderzye, ten-and-a-half miles. The rear-guard was again fired upon by a body of about fifty men crowning some little heights on the left of our line of march. No harm was done; but a camp follower, who is missing, is conjectured to have been cut off. The water is very brackish, and the villages are totally deserted.

21st. To Hykulzye, ten-and-a-half miles, a large village, the inhabitants of which had remained, under assurances of protection. They produced some supplies, which were eagerly purchased at most exorbitant rates, by our followers, who cannot possibly subsist, for any length of time, on half rations, and are consequently obliged to eke out a meal by picking up weeds and vegetables, with the nature of which they are unacquainted, and which frequently prove injurious. The Artillery horses are beginning to knock up from starvation—there being no grain, and very scanty forage only, generally of a kind to which they are unaccustomed, and which consequently disagrees with them. No fewer than seven, which had sunk from exhaustion, were shot on the line of march to day; and, within the last few days, several others also, of the Auxiliary Horse, have shared the same fate.

Despatches received from Sir John Keane's camp, dated 19th instant, inform us that the army is now united, fifteen miles beyond the Kojak pass, and that it will advance upon Candahar on the 21st, with the prospect of arriving at that city about the 25th instant, no opposition being expected. Two of the Sirdars having, however, left Candahar with a large body of horse, and gone, it was not known whither, the advance is on the alert. It had been detained several days in preparing and surmounting the Kojak pass, which is described to be about three-and-a-half miles long. The road is well made, but the many steep acclivities and descents require much manual labour to bring the guns over. It is three days since I have been permitted to leave my couch, and to sit on my chair for a short time, and I am now using crutches.

22d. Marched to a river, six-and-a-half miles distant, which we crossed; but, in consequence of the difficulty of passing guns over it, we did not advance further. A mutilated body was found on the ground. The ravines about the river, being full of crannies and fissures, afford cover to numerous banditti, who lose no opportunity of carrying off whatever they can lay their hands upon—murdering every camp follower who comes in their way. A peon, in charge of three camels that were grazing close to camp, was cut down this morning, and the camels carried off, and an officer's horse was seized when leading down to water at midday, and ridden away. Parties sent in pursuit traced the robbers to villages at no great distance, strongly situated among the ravines on the river bank, and filled with armed inhabitants. These turned out, to resist any attempts to follow the robbers to whom they had given refuge, and as neither time nor policy could authorize an attack, we were obliged to content ourselves with representing the aggression to the Envoy.

At night, I went on with Major Todd and a cavalry escort to Abdoollah Khan's fort, distant ten miles, and some three miles off the road. It is held by a regiment of the Shah's Infantry, under British officers, and is an extensive place, fortified with mud walls and round towers, which are neither provided with guns, nor pierced with embrasures. It affords good accommodation for the officers, with space sufficient to encamp a regiment, and contains also gardens of the fruit-trees common to Europe, amongst which I saw cherries already formed. The officers speak highly of the climate, and are well pleased with the place, but great anxiety is felt regarding the subsistence of their men. Whilst the Shah's Commissariate is unable to meet the demands upon it, only two days' rations of their own remain. Little hope also is entertained of obtaining supplies from the neighbourhood, the Chiefs of which are inimical to the Shah, and we ourselves are in no condition to assist them.

24th. Two severe shocks of an earthquake were felt this morning. The Artillery Brigade encamping about three miles north of the fort, I joined in the evening.—25th. Marched ten miles, to the entrance of the Kojak pass. A good road had been made for the Bengal column, but the ascents and declivities, for three-and-a-half miles, are so steep, as to present a most formidable undertaking to our artillery and jaded cattle. A portion of the baggage and of the 4th Troop of Horse Artillery were passed over during the day, with the assistance of H. M. 17th Foot and camp followers, who continued working at intervals also during the night. Bivouacked on the further side of the pass. Our baggage was frequently menaced by the hill people from the fastnesses around us, but they were well warded off by flanking parties of the 17th Regiment, by whom several were killed.

26th. The 4th Troop of Horse Artillery, and all those who had surmounted the pass, moved in the morning three miles to Chunnum, where there are some fine springs, but scarcely a blade of grass for our miserable horses, many of which were lost in the pass, owing to exhaustion caused by deficiency of food. At 9 P. M. I pushed on in advance with Major

Todd, escorted by twenty-four of the Auxiliary Horse, our baggage being guarded by fifty matchlockmen proceeding to meet the Shah. Reached Killa Futtoolah, twenty-four miles, at 7 A. M. on the 26th, shortly after the departure of the Park of the Bengal Army. Numerous natives were on the ground, picking up what the troops had left; and although they fled at our approach, they were subsequently persuaded to return. Here is the shell of a fort, but neither village nor inhabitants are to be seen for a considerable distance. The remains of cultivation are extensive, but the stream in the mountains, which served to irrigate it, having been turned by our enemies, we were much distressed for want of water.

About midday we were so fortunate as to discover a small well, but it was exhausted by evening. Employed our people in searching for water, opening wells which had been filled up, and obtaining such information as to the source of the water which had been cut off, as may, we hope, enable the Bombay Division to obtain a supply. Yesterday, for the first time since my accident, I mounted a horse, riding three miles in the morning, and the greater part of this long night march besides, with little inconvenience. Having determined, in consequence, to continue my journey entirely on horseback, I left my dooly here. On this road we passed the bodies of many murdered followers, others being also found lying about in the vicinity of our camp. Under pretence of showing them water and provisions, the natives had enticed these men, solely for the purpose of murdering them in cold blood. Information received this day that the Shah has entered Candahar without opposition.

27th. Marched at 8 A. M. to Mel-i-Nadir, thirteen miles, over a trying road for guns, very stony, with numerous ascents and descents, and no water the whole way. About two miles from our last camp, came upon an unfortunate Bengal camp follower, who, having been left on the road plundered and wounded by the natives, must soon have died, but for our timely assistance. We had, fortunately, a little water to give the poor fellow, and never did I see water so greedily swallowed. Sent back for the dooly which I had left at the last ground, and returned the man in it, under protection of a guard, to await the arrival of the troops. At Mel-i-Nadir found a stream of water, the corpses of numerous murdered followers being scattered also in this neighbourhood. Here, however, no natives showed themselves, in consequence, probably, of their being aware that the practice of enticing our people to destroy them, had become notorious. In the neighbourhood are some paltry villages, entirely deserted; but, judging from the appearance of the cultivation in our vicinity, the inhabitants must be near at hand. At 9 P. M. moved on to Tukt-i-Pool, fourteen miles, arriving there at 1 A. M., and finding the camp of the 4th Bengal Brigade and Artillery Park on the point of marching thence, we accompanied them.

28th. To Dil-i-Hadjee, a considerable village, lately plundered by the Sirdars of Candahar, who had come out thus far to oppose our army; but who, owing to dissensions among themselves, and the defection of an eminent chief, Hadji Khan Khaker, on whom they principally relied, had broken up their army and returned to Candahar, flying from that city, with scarcely two hundred followers, on the 24th instant, the day previous to the Shah's arrival. The road from Mel-i-Nadir to Dil-i-Hadjee is generally good, with the exception of a trifling pass about five miles from the former place, which was strewed with the dead bodies of our unfortunate followers; of whom one hundred are estimated to have fallen on this march alone.

29th. Joined Sir John Keane to breakfast, twenty-two miles, and found His Excellency pitched in a delightful garden, a few hundred yards from the walls of Candahar, with the different camps scattered around in various directions. The Army is in great distress for want of provisions; six days supplies only remain in the commissariate stores, and the merchants of Candahar, who profess to have nothing in reserve, retail wheat flour in small quantities, at the rate of two seers (4lb.) for the rupee, everything else being proportionally dear.

30th. Visited Mr. Macnaghten in the city, where the officers of the mission are residing in one of the palaces, a very indifferent building. The town is enclosed by a wall thirty feet in height, and is one-and-a-half miles long, by one broad. The houses are built of mud, and the streets are narrow and dirty. Hasty preparations for defence are everywhere visible around the walls in paltry outworks. Although possessing a double wall and ditch, the place could not have stood against the British Artillery above twenty-four hours, and no cannon appear on the numerous towers. Consulted Mr. Macnaghten regarding supplies, and measures were resolved upon, which we hope may relieve the wants of the army until the harvest (which promises to be plentiful, and is, it is said, already under the sickle in the southern districts) enables the commisariate to replenish its stores. This valley is covered with corn, but it cannot be ripe for a fortnight or twenty days. At least a month will be required to restore our exhausted cattle, and the horses especially; upwards of three hundred of those, in the Bengal Cavalry and Artillery alone, having already been lost; whilst the remainder are so reduced in condition, as to be barely able to move from their pickets. There exists but slender prospect of grain for the poor animals, however, so long as the wants of man continue to be thus pressing. Despatched provisions to meet the Bombay Division; to obtain which, as well as to inform General Willshire of the nature of the road in his front, (no communications from those in advance having previously been received,) were my principal reasons for preceding his Division.

CHAPTER XII.

CANDAHAR.

1st May. Cossids report that the Persians are advancing on Herat; but of this rumour there is no confirmation from Lieutenant Pottinger or other authentic sources. The Commander-in-Chief held his first levee to receive the Bengal officers, and it was attended also by Mr. Macnaghten and the gentlemen of the mission. In the evening I accompanied Sir John Keane to visit the Shah, who had sought an interview, that he might consult about relieving the wants of the army, and concert measures for the pursuit of the Sirdars, who are said to be in occupation of a fort about seventy miles on the road to Herat, and to be raising troops.

2d. An expedition was arranged to pursue the Sirdars, consisting of two companies of European Infantry, and one thousand native Infantry, three hundred Cavalry, and two guns; but, in consequence of certain overtures received from the fugitives, its march is for the present delayed.—3d. Waited on Mr. Macnaghten to arrange the programme of a military spectacle on the occasion of the Shah's first appearance in public to receive the homage of his subjects. Everything has been determined on, excepting the day, which must be fixed by his Majesty.

4th. The Bombay Division arrived, and, considering the length and difficulties of its march, was in good order, the horses of the Artillery and Auxiliary Cavalry excepted, about one hundred and fifty of which have dropped on the road from exhaustion. The survivors have suffered much, but are in a better state than the horses of the Bengal Army, three hundred and fifty of which have been lost. It is a fact now fully proved, and admitted by all parties, that the Arab and Persian horses stand their work and privations infinitely better than stud and country-breds; the latter although younger, stronger, and in far better condition at starting, having invariably been the first to give in, while they seldom rallied afterwards. A few Cape horses, lately imported to the Bombay Army, have also proved themselves superior to our stud breds. General Willshire's Brigade had had several affairs with horsemen hovering about the baggage, both before and after joining the Artillery Brigade at the Kojak pass; in which upwards of fifty of the marauders were killed, with the loss of only two or three on our side. It is estimated that at least five hundred Beloches, Khakers, and Affghans, have been slain by our troops since leaving Shikarpore and Larkhana; the loss on our side being thirty or forty killed in open combat, besides some hundreds of followers murdered.

6th. It has been determined to depute Major Todd to Herat, as Envoy, together with certain Engineer and Artillery Officers, who are to strengthen the works of that fortress prior to the advance of troops, in the event of the Shah of Persia returning to besiege it; but of this intention on his part, no authentic accounts have yet been received.

8th. In order to celebrate the restoration of Shah Shooja ool Moolk to the kingdom of his ancestors, the whole of the British Army was drawn up at dawn of day, in front of a throne, raised in the midst of an extensive plain to the north of the city. At sun-rise, the guns of the palace announced His Majesty's departure,—Sir John Keane with his Staff, awaiting the egress of the procession at the Herat gate— whence, under a salute of twenty-one guns, the King proceeded on horseback, through a street formed by his own contingent. On his ascending the musnud, the whole line presented arms, whilst a salvo was discharged from one hundred and one pieces of artillery. The Army of the Indus then marched round; in front of the throne, in order of review, mustering seven thousand men of all arms, and presenting a most imposing spectacle. In the evening I attended the Commander-in-Chief to the residence of the Envoy, who gave an entertainment in honor of the King's accession, when appropriate speeches were delivered by Sir John Keane, by Mr. Macnaghten, and Sir Alexander Burnes. On our return through the city, the few lamps that had been lighted, in a poor attempt to illuminate the streets, had become totally extinguished.*

* Not having been present at the entrance of Shah Shooja ool Moolk into Candahar, I extract from the Bom-

9th. The Sirdars having rejected the terms which
bay papers of June 1839, the following description from the
pen of an officer who witnessed it:—

"On the morning of the 24th April, the King approached Candahar, but without any intention of marching into the city. The scarcity of water, however, compelled His Majesty to approach within three miles. The British Army was in the rear. The King was even in advance of his own troops. The morning had scarcely dawned, when parties of horse were discovered—they were soon ascertained to be friends, come to pay their duty to their sovereign. They gallopped up, dismounted, drew up in line, prayed for the King, who welcomed them, and then fell into the rear of the procession. One standard after another thus joined the King, and, ere His Majesty had reached Candahar, he had been joined by about one thousand five hundred well mounted, dressed, and caparisoned horse. Mr. Macnaghten and the officers of his mission, with a small honorary escort, were alone in attendance, of the British force. On His Majesty's entry into the city, there could not have been less than between sixty and seventy thousand persons present. The balconies were crowded with women—the streets lined with men,—and from all quarters a universal shout of welcome was heard. The exclamations were " Candahar is gained from the Baruckzyes," "May your power endure for ever," "We look to you for protection," " May your enemies be destroyed," " Son of Timour Shah, you are welcome." Flowers and loaves of bread were cast before his Majesty.—After passing through the city, the King dismounted from his horse, and proceeded to the shrine containing the shirt of the Prophet, and offered up thanksgivings; thence he went to the tomb of his grandfather, and prayed. On both these occasions he was accompanied by the British Envoy, and the Officers of his Suite. The party returned through the city with the same demonstrations of loyalty and respect on the part of the populace; and the eventful day passed over without any accident."

had been offered to them, the detachment previously prepared, is ordered to march under Brigadier Sale upon Girishk. It is expected that on the approach of this force, the Sirdárs, who have now no more than one hundred followers, will either fly or submit.—10th. In consequence of the dearness of wheat flour, which has risen to 1½ seers (3lbs.) per rupee, our camp followers are reduced to the greatest distress. It has at length, therefore, been determined to extend to them the indulgence of half rations, which the followers of the Bengal Army have long enjoyed.—11th. A riot at the city gates, and several merchants plundered; a circumstance not to be wondered at, driven by want, as our followers are, to desperation. To me it is only surprising that, under the hardships and privations, to which they have been subjected, they should so long have abstained from helping themselves.

12th. Some twenty followers, who were yesterday apprehended in the act of carrying away property, which had been plundered during the riot, were flogged at the gates of the city. In consideration of the extreme distress, to which the camp followers are reduced, and of this being the first offence of the sort, since the landing of our army in Sinde, the capital punishment, usually awarded on such occasions, has been in this instance remitted. Reports received from Cabul, stating that the adherents of Dost Mahommed Khan had deserted to the Shah's son at Peshawur, and that the ex-Ruler is disposing of his property and supplies, preparatory to his seeking an asylum in Bokhara, when our army shall advance.

This morning the expedition marched against Girishk, whence it is expected that the Sirdars will retreat into Persia, in preference to submitting to our terms. A letter intercepted, which had been despatched to Dost Mahommed Khan by one of his secret agents. After describing our late review, and assuring the fallen chief that instead of the myriads of soldiers we had been represented to possess, the British Army consists of no more than two thousand five hundred Cavalry, and seven thousand Infantry, the writer concludes his epistle by exhorting the Khan to be of good courage—to advance and oppose us! No intelligence having been received from Herat, since our arrival at Candahar, it is conjectured that the Sirdars occupying Girishk, which fortress is on the direct road, must have intercepted our letters.

Provisions are daily becoming scarcer, and more dear, and flour has actually attained the exorbitant rate of a single seer for a rupee; a price which is of course quite beyond the means of our impoverished followers. No grain has yet been obtained for the horses, nor are they thriving on the green forage which is now procurable; but the barley, to which we look for their restoration, is already being reaped, and, most fortunately, the crops of wheat will also soon be ready for the harvest. The weather during the day is now becoming excessively oppressive— the thermometer ranging in our tents from 100° to 110°, but the nights are still cool and pleasant. Generally speaking, the troops continue to be healthy; but the effects of the unwholesome food, which the wretched followers have been obliged to consume, is everywhere painfully manifest.

* * * *
* * * *

[My journal from the 13th of May to the 14th of June has been lost. During that period the Army was halted before Candahar, and nothing of interest occurred, saving the occupation of Girishk which was quietly relinquished into the hands of General Sale's detachment by the Sirdars, who, on the approach of the British, fled with precipitation to the frontiers of Persia. On the 15th of June the army was still before Candahar.]

15th June. Accounts received from Cabul state, that Dost Mahommed Khan, who had been deceived, by our long delay here, into the belief, that that city would not be attempted until next year—and who, conceiving that our attention would first be directed towards Herat, had posted a portion of his army at Jullabad above the Khyber pass, with a design of checking the troops of the Shahzadah and the Seiks, —is now, on learning our real intentions, in the greatest alarm. It is said that he is pressing the people to labour on the defences of Ghizni, and that he has disgusted the inhabitants of that fortress by destroying their orchards and vineyards in order to clear the approaches;—that he distrusts all about him, and not long since, having assembled all his chiefs and followers, endeavoured to exact an oath of allegiance, which, however, they refused to take, on the grounds, that from such faithful adherents it was altogether unnecessary. A clearer proof that they are open to seduction, could scarcely be given. The ex-Ruler has deputed one of his sons to effect certain arrangements with the Ghiljee tribes for our obstruction through their territories. In consequence of the non-arrival of the kafila expected two days ago, the advance of the army, which had been ordered to take place to-day, has been further delayed.

16th. In the absence of cash, all commissariate purchases are suspended. Upwards of thirty lakhs of Rupees have been disbursed in this city; but every attempt to negociate a loan has failed; and although the convoy, which is daily expected, left Shikarpore so late as the 3d. instant, ten lakhs of Rupees, which were forwarded thence on the 23d. ultimo, have not yet arrived.—17th. We are beginning to feel the effects of the hostility of the Ghiljees, who evidently understand how to deal with us, and daily contrive to carry off camels from the grazing ground in the neighbourhood of our camp. Ten, belonging to Major Leach, were stolen this morning; and the Shah, hoping, by severe example, to check the evil, has caused to be blown away from a gun, a Ghiljee, who, in an attempt upon our camels, had killed a camel-man, and wounded a trooper of the Cavalry.

18th. The Envoy informed the Commander-in-Chief, that the Ghiljees are bent on hostilities, and have assembled, either with the design of attacking our advanced Cavalry picquet, some fourteen miles hence, or of cutting off the convoy which is advancing in the rear. Orders have consequently been sent to the former to fall back if menaced; and a detachment consisting of a Regiment of Bengal Cavalry, a Regiment of Bengal Infantry, and two guns, has been ordered out to meet and protect the latter. —19th. The heads of four Affghans, who have been slain in an attempt upon our camels, were brought into camp.—20th. The whole of the camels, upwards of one hundred and fifty in number, belonging to H. M.'s 13th Regiment, were carried off whilst grazing close to the camp; one of five unarmed Europeans in charge of them being killed, and the other four severely wounded. A party of horse and foot sent out immediately in pursuit, was unfortunately not in time to overtake the bandits.— 21st. Died Dr. Hamilton, H. M.'s 17th Foot. In consequence of a reported movement on the part of the Ghiljees to intercept the long expected convoy, a regiment of Infantry with a squadron of Cavalry, has been ordered to meet it by a route differing from that adopted by the detachment which marched on the 18th instant.

23d. The convoy arrived in safety, the Ghiljees having been deterred from shewing themselves by the strong reinforcement so seasonably sent out. It would seem that the kafila had been secretly joined, on this side of Quetta, by some of the emissaries of Dost Mahommed Khan, who had endeavoured to seduce its director, Sirwa Khan, the Lohanee chief, and his followers, to desert our cause, and carry over the convoy to the ex-Ruler. These agents had actually succeeded in alienating a number of the followers; and had the chief himself remained faithful, of which there is some reason to doubt, they would probably have so far undermined his influence as to have gained over the whole convoy to the enemy, but for the determined conduct of a party of the Bengal Horse, who declared their determination of opposing such treachery with their lives; and maintained day and night so vigilant a guard, that the scale was turned, and one of the emissaries was seized, and brought into camp a prisoner. Much opposition had been experienced in the Bolan and Kojak passes from the predatory hordes, who had plundered and wounded many members of the kafila. This morning the Shah shifted his camp, preparatory to the march; but our advance, which was to have taken place the day after the arrival of the convoy, is again delayed, in consequence of an objection on the part of Sirwa Khan to employ his camels further. By transporting his charge to the army, he has fulfilled his contract; but without his continued assistance the army cannot now be equipped with full rations.

24th. Four days having been lost, in fruitless endeavours to overcome the objections of Sirwa Khan, we shall be compelled to advance without the aid of his kafila, and to carry half rations only for a single month.

CHAPTER XIII.

MARCH FROM CANDAHAR TO GHIZNI.

27th June. The advance column and the Head Quarters marched from Candahar, and passing the Shah's camp two miles from the City, encamped four miles beyond it, at Abdool Azeez.—28th. At 2 A. M. marched to Killa-i-Azeem, nineteen miles, where the water was very brackish. A Ghiljee chief, attended by forty or fifty horsemen, passed our camp on his way to tender his submission to the Shah, after delaying so to do until the moment of our actually advancing upon Cabul. It is said that another chief, with a large proportion of the Ghiljees, has gone off to join Dost Mahommed Khan; but the disunion, which has already taken place amongst that tribe, must in a great measure relieve us from the harassing depredations to, which our baggage would otherwise have been exposed.

29th. Killa-i-Akhoond, sixteen miles, on the right bank of the Turnuk river. After five miles, the road leaves the valley of Candahar, which is perfectly level; but at this season, inconsequence of the extensive crops having been harvested, is quite destitute of verdure, save such as is afforded by patches of scanty camel forage. Quitting this valley, the road leads through a range of hills by various acclivities and descents, to the valley of the Turnuk, a small stream, the banks of which are skirted by extensive cultivation.

30th. Encamped again on the Turnuk, at Shervi Suffer, twelve miles in advance. About three miles from our ground, the road being confined for a few hundred yards between the river and a trivial range of hills, was too narrow to admit of the passage of Artillery, but by the united exertion of the Bengal sappers and pioneers, it was speedily rendered practicable.

1st July. Marched ten miles to Teer Undaz on the Turnuk, the road flooded in many places by the Ghiljees, who had hoped by this means to retard the advance of our army, but the difficulties were nevertheless overcome. Accounts received this day from Killa-i-Ghiljee, state, that the Ghiljees are assembling in great force; that they already muster at that place about one thousand men, and expect reinforcements to the amount of six thousand more. It is not probable that they will oppose us openly, but a chuppao may be expected, or they may scatter in small bands, and menacing our long line of baggage, harass our followers, and carry off our cattle whilst grazing. To this calling together of the clans we may attribute our having been hitherto unmolested, except in the single instance where the Shah lost one hundred and sixty of his camels. These were probably taken by the party of Ghiljees who passed our camp on the 28th ultimo; who never fulfilled their avowed intention of joining the King, while the robbery took place that very night.

2nd. Advanced ten-and-a-half miles to Khoor, on the Turnuk. On the march the army was detained two hours whilst a difficult pass was being cleared for the guns.—3rd. Encamped again on the banks of the Turnuk, ten miles, in advance, amongst corn-fields still uncut. This is a proof of the elevation of our present position above the valley of Candahar, in which the crops were reaped upwards of a month ago. My tent being unfortunately pitched on the bank of the river in a very exposed situation, with no sentry near it, I suffered a severe loss. Two of my horses were stolen from their picquets during the night by the Ghiljees, who are notoriously expert, and did not in this instance disturb the horse-keepers, although they were both actually sleeping at the feet of the horses. One of the animals, my chestnut Arab charger, was without exception the finest in the whole army, and at this juncture especially, was to me invaluable. Sir Alexander Burnes has, in the hope of recovering him, offered on my behalf the sum of two thousand rupees, to the person who may, at any price, succeed in effecting his ransom, and several natives of the country have already set out for the purpose of endeavouring to earn this reward.

4th. Marched twelve miles to Killa-i-Ghiljee, a steep and isolated hill, formerly fortified—the modern village in the plain, about a mile off, being, however, a very paltry place. Excepting a few mounted scouts, who fled at our approach, we observed no signs of the Ghiljees, and after our arrival proposals of submission were sent in by one of the Chiefs. We still drink the waters of the Turnuk, which flows about two miles from the village.—5th. Halted. The Shah and the Envoy joined our camp from the rear. The Ghiljee Chiefs Abdool Rehman, and Gool Mahommed, having refused to submit to the King's authority, two other leading members of the tribe have been set up as rulers in their stead. No measure having, however, yet been adopted to extract the sting of the disaffected Chiefs, it is not to be expected that they will quietly submit to the arrangement made. Their wrath will doubtless be wreaked upon such of our unfortunate followers as may fall into their hands, and in earnest of this, two of the latter were murdered yesterday, and another this morning.

6th. Encamped at Sir-i-usp, on the Turnuk, ten miles, the road to it being tolerably good, a few obstacles to the advance of guns excepted, which were easily cleared away by the pioneers.—7th. Leaving the Turnuk, we struck across undulating hillocks to Nouruk, nine-and-a-half miles, where the road again approaches the river, and leads to our present encamping ground on its banks. Here the stream is extremely rapid, and far deeper than we had hitherto found it, numerous rills carrying off the water for the purposes of irrigation.—8th. Advanced to Tazee, nine miles, over a road similar to that traversed yesterday, and encamped again on the Turnuk, where fish are abundant. Within the last few days, the

Ghiljees have succeeded in abstracting a few of the straying camels, and it is supposed that some of the missing followers have been murdered by them. To-day, in an attempt made on our camels, a Ghiljee was killed, and some others were made prisoners.—9th. Certain obstructions on the road, which the sappers and miners have been sent to remove, having obliged us to halt, the Shah's camp has overtaken us.

10th. Moved six-and-a-quarter miles, to Shaftal, still on the bank of the Turnuk, at a distance from either village or cultivation. At night two troopers were attacked and robbed within the picquets by some of our own camp followers, and one of them was murdered.—11th. Marched ten-and-a-half miles to Chushma-i-Shadee. Abdool Rehman, one of the principal Ghiljee chiefs, this day tendered his submission, but on such impudent conditions that no answer has been returned to him.—12th. Chusma-i-Punjah, seven miles, encamping at some springs two miles to the left of the Turnuk. In consequence of a report that the Ghiljee chief, Abdool Rehman, is in our neighbourhood with five hundred horse, a reconnoissance was ordered, but nothing was seen of the enemy. Accounts from the Bombay Brigade, two days in our rear, state, that two attempts have been made on their camels, and that numerous murdered followers are daily found in our track.

13th. Encamped at Ghozan, twelve miles, on a stream of clear water, running across the plain. The road level and good through the valley, which has increased to ten and fifteen miles in breadth; the foot of the hills on both sides being studded with small fortified villages. In an endeavour to rescue some camels that had been captured by the Ghiljees, two of the 4th Local Horse were killed, one of the bandits being also slain, and another taken prisoner. —14th. Reached the source of the Turnuk river, the course of which, running parallel to our line of march, is marked by numerous little forts, constructed within musket shot of each other. Encamped at Mokoos, twelve-and-a-half miles, on a smooth green turf. During this march, some baggage was plundered, and seven stragglers were butchered. Accounts from the rear state that the Shah's Affghans have surprised a body of Ghiljees, killing many, and capturing one standard, with the loss of several slain and wounded.

15th. Halted. The Shah arrived. During his Majesty's last march, his flanks had been assailed by numerous Ghiljee plunderers, of whom many were mounted; others on foot occupied a range of hills commanding the road: of these latter, thirteen were killed by the Shah's Goorkah Battalion, in an attack which ended in their dispersion.—16th. Marched fourteen-and-a-half miles to Oba, by an excellent road across a level plain, the valley still widening as we advanced, and the hills on both sides skirted by innumerable small forts, surrounded by cultivation. A native was shot by the sentence of a Drum-head Court Martial, for wounding and robbing some of the camp followers.

17th. To Kurabagh, twelve-and-a-half miles, over a road similar to that of yesterday. The accounts from Cabul and Ghizni have hitherto been most conflicting as to the proceedings of Dost Mahommed Khan, but it now appears certain that his eldest son has, with four guns, reinforced the Governor of Ghizni, his younger brother, who has already eight pieces of Artillery, while the troops assembled in that fortress, the ancient capital of Affghanistan, are said to amount to two thousand horse, and the like number of foot; and it is confidently stated, that the Khan himself marched yesterday from Cabul, *en route* to place himself at their head. The disaffected Ghiljee chiefs are reported to be moving with a considerable body of cavalry on our flanks, intending either to aid the Khan in resisting our advance, or, in the event of no opposition being offered on his part, to tender their submission to the British. Heavy rain fell during the night.

18th. Advanced nine miles to Moshakee. On the mountains to our left snow was observable, and on both sides of the valley, among flourishing cultivation, were scattered numerous little forts and villages. The road, although crossed by several artificial water-courses, was good. Authentic accounts being here received that the enemy have assembled in force to oppose us at Ghizni, orders have been despatched, directing the columns in the rear to close up by forced marches. Another heavy fall of rain during the night.

19th. Marched by a very heavy and stony, though level road to Urghesan, nine-and-a-half miles, the second column, with the Shah, joining us there during the day. On our advanced guard reaching the ground, it was fired upon by a patrol of about fifty of the enemy's horse, who, after a few shots, were driven into the hills.

20th. To Azga-Name, eight-and-a-half miles, through a more open country, no further hostile indications being made on the part of the enemy, although the minarets of Ghizni are now actually in sight. At midnight we were joined by General Willshire's Brigade; and in consequence of information having been received of an intended *chuppao* upon the camp, we were kept all night on the alert.

21st. The whole army, arranged in three columns, moved over the intermediate spacious plain, and reached Ghizni after a march of about twelve miles. No appearance whatever of an enemy was observable until within a mile of the fort, when on our approaching some walled gardens, scouts were perceived to be hastily evacuating them. The Commander-in-Chief and staff, having passed the gardens, awaited the arrival of the troops, in a position overlooking the fort; observing which, the enemy opened a few guns from the walls, discharging also several matchlocks from a garden in our vicinity. On the arrival of the Infantry, a party of skirmishers, having been thrown into this garden, cleared it with little opposition, and our artillery was then placed in position, about seven hundred yards from the walls. As a demonstration, and with a design of ascertaining the strength of the enemy's guns, our batteries were then opened; but, after a few rounds, our fire was discontinued, although not until the explosion of some of our shells within the crowded bastions had been attended with considerable effect.

The fort now opened seven or eight guns in return, whilst a brisk and well-directed fire was kept up from numerous gingals and wall pieces. In the meantime, the Light Companies of the 35th, and 48th Regiments of Bengal Native Infantry, which were in occupation of the gardens, had been warmly engaged with the Garrison of one of the principal outworks, and the skirmishing continued until I was sent down by the Commander-in-Chief to prohibit their further exposure. Both the guns and troops having then been withdrawn out of range, a reconnoissance was made, the report of which caused us to shift our camp in the evening to the south-eastern side of the fortress, on the road to Cabul. In consequence of a demonstration on the part of the enemy's Cavalry, who had threatened to turn our flank, with the design of attacking the baggage, the Bombay Cavalry and Infantry Brigade had been halted when within about three miles of the fort, in order to afford protection to our rear. Throughout this day, the casualties on our side were limited to two officers wounded, and ten or twelve men, besides five or six horses, killed and wounded; the principal loss being sustained by the Light Companies before mentioned.

During the time that the Commander-in-Chief was passing through the gardens towards his first position, I proceeded in advance, and examined the road between the enclosure marked 1. 1. in the plan, as far as the village, where I had the honour of eliciting the first shot from the fort; and I afterwards brought up a squadron of the Lancers to support His Excellency until the arrival of the Force. I was subsequently despatched by Sir John Keane to halt the Bombay Infantry, for the protection of the baggage, which was threatened as above related, and, for the same reason, to order the Bombay Cavalry Brigade to fall back in support. On my rejoining the head-quarters, the Artillery were cannonading from the commanding ridge marked 2. 3. whilst the Bengal Light Infantry, occupying the garden 5, were engaged with the garrison of the redoubt 6, as already narrated.

Whilst delivering to the officer commanding the Light Companies the orders with which I had been charged by his Excellency, the fire of the Garrison—at this point not sixty yards distant—was so hot and well directed, that few of the skirmishers showed their heads above the walls with impunity; and those walls, which in some measure screened them, affording me no protection whatever, had I even been able to obtain access to them, I may consider myself fortunate in having been able to deliver my orders without interruption. Judging from my limited military experience, I am of opinion that the opposition offered by the Affghans was highly creditable; nor can it be deemed astonishing that the greater portion of to-day's casualties, few though they be, should have occurred here.

CHAPTER XIV.

THE STORM OF GHIZNI.

22d July. At break of day, the Commander-in-Chief ascended the heights on the right of our camp, which completely command the eastern face of the works, and having thence reconnoitred the fortress, His Excellency has resolved upon making the attempt to carry it by storm to-morrow. The assault is to be directed against the Cabul gate, which it is proposed to blow open by means of bags of loose gunpowder, that are to be attached, if possible, before daylight, failing in which, the object must be effected by Artillery. By a false attack on the opposite quarter, the attention of the enemy is to be diverted, and his fire is to be in some measure kept down by batteries, which are to be established, after nightfall, on the commanding heights.

The storming party is to consist of four companies of Europeans, under Brigadier Dennie, and the assaulting column to be composed of the remainder of the four European Regiments, under Brigadier Sale, with three Regiments of Native Infantry in reserve. The garrison being resolute, and the fortifications far stronger than we had been led to anticipate, it cannot of course be expected that the capture will be achieved without considerable loss ; but whilst the delay arising from the operations of a regular siege would be, under existing circumstances, extremely hazardous, our limited means, in respect to Artillery especially, render such a mode of proceeding impracticable. The enemy's Cavalry, commanded by one of the sons of the Ameer Dost Mahommed Khan, having been joined by the disaffected Ghiljee Chiefs, are conjectured to muster upwards of three thousand sabres. They are now watching a favourable opportunity to fall upon our camp, and their advanced picquets were observed this morning to the northward. Dost Mahommed Khan himself is reported to be advancing from the Cabul side, and is expected to arrive to-morrow, though with what amount of force is not known. His direct communication with the fort, however, is cut off by our present position.

About noon, the hills to the southward of our camp were crowned by masses of horse and foot, displaying several standards ; their designs appearing to be directed against the Shah's camp, which lay immediately under their position. Two of his Majesty's guns, with all his Cavalry, supported by Lancers, and by a Regiment of Bengal Cavalry, moved out immediately to oppose this demonstration ; and the enemy, who had already began to descend into the plain, being met by the Shah's Horse, under Captain Nicolson, were, with trivial loss on our side, compelled to re-ascend the heights, leaving behind

one of their standards in our possession, and four or
five of their number killed in the conflict. Having
gallopped out to ascertain what was going on, I reached the scene of action just before this occurrence; and,
finding no European officer on the spot, I prevailed
on a body of the Shah's Horse to follow me round
the hills in the enemy's rear, where I stationed them
so as to cut off their retreat. The enemy, being
intimidated by this movement, and repulsed by
Captain Nicolson's gallant charge, ascended the
heights beyond all reach of our Horse, whom I
therefore left in position, returning myself to the
front.

Meeting at this juncture a small detachment of
the Shah's contingent, consisting of about one
hundred and fifty infantry and matchlock-men, under a European officer, I suggested to him the
propriety of an immediate attempt to force the enemy
from the heights, in the direction where I had just
stationed the Cavalry. He expressed his readiness
to act under my orders; and, relinquishing to me
the charge of his detachment, which was composed
of picquets from different corps hastily assembled,
we ascended the hill together. The matchlock-men
behaved with great gallantry, advancing steadily
under a galling fire, and availing themselves of every
rock and stone, as fast as the enemy were dislodged.
They were followed by the Sepoys in close order,
who occupied every favourable undulation of ground,
and were thus prepared to meet any sudden rush
that might be made on the part of the enemy. Step
by step, we thus at last attained the loftiest peak,

over the crest of which floated the holy banner of
green and white,—the largest and most conspicuous
in the ranks of the whole host, the first unfurling of
which, by the Moslem High Priest, who had preached
a crusade against the British, had called together a
mob of fanatics, who, judging from their reckless
personal exposure, must have been deceived into the
belief that they were safe under the charm of its
sacred influence. Towards this object we made
our way, ascending a very precipitous acclivity, under a smart fire, from which we were sheltered by
the rocks, until, on our arriving within fifty paces of
the enemy, a fortunate shot brought down the stand-
ard-bearer. The whole of our party then rushing
up with a general cheer, the banner was seized,
whilst the enemy, panic-stricken at this proof of the
fallacy of their belief, fled with precipitation to a
second hill, whither I deemed it useless to follow
them, both because our men were already much
exhausted from thirst and fatigue, and because the
range, instead of terminating, as I had conjectured,
at this point, in which case the fugitives might easily
have been driven into the plain—proved to be a succession of steep hills, among which it was not practicable for Cavalry to act.

Having rested some time, therefore, we finally
retired, bearing off our wounded, nine or ten in
number, and leaving the bodies of five of our
opponents lying around the spot on which the large
standard had been planted. Ten or twelve others,
who had fallen in the contest towards that position,
were likewise strewed on the face of the hill, making

a total loss, on the side of the enemy, of thirty or forty killed and wounded, in addition to about fifty made prisoners by the Cavalry: one of these latter, on being brought into the King's presence, stabbed one of the principal officers of state in the open durbar—an offence for which the whole are said to have atoned with their lives. On our side the total loss, throughout this affair, amounted to about twenty in killed and wounded.

23d July. By 3 A. M. the various detachments were at their respective posts, and all the guns in position at points which commanded the eastern face, as well as the Cabul gate of the fortress. So quietly and judiciously were these arrangements effected, that not a single shot had been elicited from the garrison, until, at last, they were aroused from their fancied security by the false attack made upon the the opposite quarter. The storming party, led by Colonel Dennie, then rushed up the Cabul gate, where they opened a fire upon the parapets which commanded the entrance, whilst Captains Thompson and Peat, with two other officers of Engineers, attached the powder-bags to the gate. These, exploding, burst it open, and, ere the garrison could recover from the astonishment into which they were thrown, Colonel Dennie, at the head of the storming party, rushed in.

An attempt was afterwards made by the enemy, to recover the lost gateway, and a large party of them for a moment actually occupied it in rear of the storming party, until the advance column, under General Sale, consisting of the remainder of the four

European Regiments, closing up to its support, the Affghans were once more dislodged, though several officers and many men, chiefly of the 2d, or Queen's Royal Regiment, were wounded in the struggle. Ere it was broad daylight, our troops were in complete possession of the lower town, the garrison descending from the walls, and effecting their escape, in every direction, no attempt being made on their part to dispute the citadel, above the bastions of which the British colours floated before the sun rose.

The capture of the strong fortress of Ghizni was thus accomplished within three-quarters of an hour from the commencement of the assault, the British loss being surprisingly small, considering that much individual gallantry was displayed in its defence, and that a heavy fire was opened on the columns of attack the moment the garrison ascertained their intention and direction. In the absence of the official returns,* I would estimate the total loss on our side, from first to last, at about fifteen officers and one hundred and twenty men wounded, in addition to about twenty men killed. The darkness, which prevailed during the conflict, being more favourable to the assailants than to the besieged, the latter suffered most severely: every street was strewed with the slain—not fewer than five hundred having been killed within the walls, and fifty-eight alone having fallen in the attempt to defend one fortified house against a company of H. M.'s 17th Foot. Numbers

* Vide Appendix.

also of the fugitives were cut up by the Cavalry, upwards of fifty being killed by the 1st Bombay Light Cavalry alone, with the loss only of one havildar killed, and six troopers wounded.

The place of every one having been previously assigned to him, and no error on the part of the columns of attack calling for His Excellency's interference during the assault, the personal Staff of the Commander-in-Chief had very little employment. I was, however, so fortunate as to be twice despatched (from the point marked A in the plan) to ascertain the progress of our operations : in the first instance, as to the effect produced by the explosion of the powder-bags on the Cabul gateway,—the entrance of our troops by which, I had the pleasure to be the first to announce to Sir John Keane ;—and again, to learn the cause of a temporary check, which, in consequence of the extreme darkness of the night, could not be comprehended. Arriving at the gate, at the moment when the supporting column was forcing its way in, I ascertained, from the officers at its head, that, although a slight check had occurred, in the manner related above, the gate had been again cleared by the troops, who were then in uninterrupted progress.

I was afterwards directed by His Excellency to place guns (at the point 7) to command the western face of the fortress, over the walls of which a number of the garrison were making their escape; and, having performed this duty, I rode round the eastern walls, to draw on a squadron of the Lancers, in order to intercept the escape of the garrison by the gardens (marked 8. 8.) Whilst passing under the walls, a large body of the enemy, who were descending by the fallen tower 9, through a breach which had not before been observed, deterred by my sudden appearance, turned back, when a picquet was planted, by which egress was precluded.

After the fall of Ghizni, its Governor, Mahommed Hyder Khan, the son of the Ameer Dost Mahommed Khan, was discovered concealed in a tower, with about twenty of his adherents; nor would the latter surrender until assured that the life of their chief should be spared. So many as fifteen or sixteen hundred prisoners have fallen into our hands, together with upwards of eight hundred horses— our soldiers having also destroyed many other horses, in self-defence, numbers gallopping loose about the streets of the town, and being withal so wild and furious, that they were even more formidable than their Affghan masters. The fortress contained abundance of ordnance and commissariate stores, and eight or nine guns, amongst which latter was a huge brass 62-pr.

A few desperate characters continued, during the whole day, to defend isolated houses, thereby wounding one officer, and killing and wounding several of the men; but, before evening, they had been all subdued, and the place was entirely cleared of the garrison. It appears that Mahommed Ubzul Khan, eldest of the sons of Dost Mahommed Khan, who had long been hovering about our neighbourhood, approached our camp, in the dark, this morning, with a large body of horse, intending to make an attack:

our fire on the fort opening at the same moment, however, the Prince stood aloof until the day dawned, when, seeing the British colours waving over the towers of the citadel, he hastily fled towards Cabul, abandoning his elephants, and the whole of his baggage, at a village about three coss distant, whither the Shah has despatched a party to take possession of them.

24th. This morning I accompanied the Commander-in-Chief to the fort, where everything is still in great confusion, the streets being strewed, in all directions, with the dead. At least five hundred of the garrison must have fallen, exclusive of those slain in the pursuit, after the place fell. Several camp followers, who had gained access to the town through a breach in one of the towers, being observed in the act of plundering, His Excellency directed that all, who might be caught, should be severely flogged.

25th. The leader of the party, which continued firing upon our soldiers, on the 23rd instant, after the town had surrendered, and who twice renewed hostilities, after having actually sued for quarter, was this day shot by order of the Commander-in-Chief. On the 28th instant, His Excellency intends resuming his march towards Cabul, designing, if possible, to reach that capital by eight marches. A small garrison will be left in occupation of Ghizni, together with the sick and wounded of the army. The latter are to be placed in the citadel, which, being an airy and spacious building, is admirably calculated for a hospital.

28th. Messengers have arrived from Cabul, who

state, that JubbulKhan Nuwab is on his way to the British camp, and will arrive, this evening, with overtures on the part of Dost Mahommed Khan, his brother. These *avant-couriers* state, that, on learning the fate of Ghizni, which had, hitherto, been looked upon as perfectly impregnable, the ex-ruler assembled his chiefs, and, after declaring his conviction that the disaster had arisen solely from treachery, commanded those among them, who designed to act towards him with duplicity, to withdraw at once. To this they all replied that they were true to his cause, and would support him against the British, but could not help suspecting an intention on his own part to desert them. The Prince, who, with the Douranee Cavalry, fled, after the fall of Ghizni, is stated to have written to Dost Mahommed Khan, assigning the loss of his baggage, and military stores, as the cause of his own retreat towards Cabul, and of his inability to resist the British; whereupon his immediate halt was directed by his father, who peremptorily refused to receive him.

29th. The Nuwab Jubbul Khan departed, after having had an interview with the King, who received him with much condescension. On being informed that the banishment to India of Dost Mahommed Khan must form one of the conditions of the treaty, the ambassador, who had spoken his mind very freely, declared, without hesitation, that the Ameer was not prepared to subscribe to any such terms; and, having then declared his own determination to follow the fortunes of his brother, he demanded, and received, his dismissal. A party of Kuzzilbashes came over to the Shah from Cabul, deserters from the standard of Dost Mahommed Khan, whom they represent to have moved out at the head of his army to Meidan, a march on this side of the capital.

CHAPTER XV.

THE PURSUIT OF DOST MAHOMMED KHAN.

The army of the Indus resumed its march towards Cabul, on the 30th July, leaving the Bombay Brigade to follow it with Shah Shooja ool Moolk, and his contingent. On the 1st and 2d of August we advanced two marches to Hyderzye, halting on the 3d to enable his Majesty to overtake us.

Authentic accounts having here been received of the flight of the Ameer Dost Mahommed Khan towards Bamian, and the abandonment of his Artillery at Meidan, two thousand of the Shah's Affghans, under Hadji Khan Kakur, or, as he was officially styled, Nusseer-ood-Dowlah,* were ordered to proceed in pursuit; the under-named British officers, with one hundred of our own cavalry, regular and irregular, volunteering to accompany the party under my orders, for the purpose of stimulating their exertions, and checking the commission of barbarities, in the event of the fugitive and his family falling into our hands. Captain Wheeler, Major of Brigade,

---

* The Defender of the State.

Bengal Cavalry Brigade; Captain Backhouse, M. B. Bengal Artillery Brigade: Captain Troup, M. B. Shah's contingent; Captain Christie, Commanding Regt. Shah's Cavalry; Captain Lawrence, Bengal Cavalry; Lieutenant Ryves, Adjutant 4th Local Horse; Captain Keith Erskine, Poona Auxiliary Horse; Lieutenant Broadfoot, Shah's Goorkah Battalion; Lieutenant Hogg, Bombay Staff; and Doctor Worral, Local Horse.

At 4 P. M. our party assembled, according to orders, at the tents of the Envoy, where the Affghans were also to have been in readiness; but, although we waited until dark, not more than three hundred effective men could be mustered, the residue of those present consisting of from four to five hundued Affghan rabble, mounted upon yaboos and starved ponies. It was however stated, that all who were still deficient would shortly follow, and our detail was for the present reinforced by one hundred of Captain Christie's horse. Hadji Khan Kakur was extremely desirous that we should pursue the high road as far as Meidan, in order to take up the track of the fugitive thence; nor was it until I had repeatedly urged upon him the obvious impossibility of our ever, by such a mode of proceeding, overtaking Dost Mahommed Khan, who had already obtained a start of twenty-four hours, that he would ultimately consent to furnish guides, who were instructed to lead us across the hills by the nearest route, so as to intersect that of the Ameer about three marches beyond Meidan.

We marched during the first night about thirty-two miles, crossing several ranges of hills, and winding along the channels of many rivers, until 7 A. M. when we reached Goda, a small village situated in a confined but fertile valley. But, although several halts had been made, in order to admit of the stragglers closing up, not more than one hundred of the Affghans had arrived with us; the rest dropping in during the day, bearing unequivocal evidence of the cause of their detention, in the plunder with which they were laden.

4th. Resumed our march in the evening, Hadji Khan being, however, most reluctant to advance. The road, which was extremely bad, wound along the channels of mountain torrents, and the face of precipitous hills. After proceeding ten miles, we bivouacked until 2 o'clock, when the moon having risen, we pushed on again until 7 A. M. of the 5th, surmounting the Pugman range by a lofty and precipitous pass, and finally encamping at a small village called Kadur-i-Suffeid, which, however, afforded no food for the people beyond parched corn. Barely fifty of the Affghans came up with us, but the rest straggled in before evening. Information being here received that Dost Mahommed Khan was at the village of Yourt, one march in our front, Hadji Khan became urgent to halt, in order that we might send back for a reinforcement, declaring that the Ameer, who has upwards of two thousand followers, is far too strong to be encountered by our present force, with any chance of a successful issue.

Having insisted, however, upon going on, I ordered a muster of the Affghans at 4 P. M. but waited until sun-set before they could be assembled, in all to the number of about seven hundred and fifty, not more than three hundred of these being mounted on war horses. With extreme difficulty, and after much altercation, these were at length induced to proceed, with the prospect of overtaking the fugitive in the morning at Hurzar, his next halt beyond Yourt; but whether through accident or design, we had not advanced four miles, before the guides, who were under the charge of Hadji Khan's men, were reported to have deserted. It was then pitch-dark, and being left in the midst of interminable ravines, where no trace even of a foot-path existed, we had no alternative but to halt until day-break, and did not in consequence reach Yourt until 7 A. M. of the following day, the 6th. At this time few of the Affghans were forthcoming, and no arguments could at first prevail on Hadji Khan to advance sixteen miles further to Hurzar, where we had positive intelligence of the presence of the object of our pursuit. At length, however, he was induced to promise most solemnly, that he would press on in the evening, and, as some consolation for the present delay, we now entertained hopes of being enabled to beat up the Ameer's quarters during the night.

Having mounted, according to previous agreement, at 4. P. M. we proceeded to the tent of Hadji Khan Kakur, with the view of ascertaining the reason that the Affghans were not prepared. He now entered into a long story, setting forth the hardships endured by his men, who, in the absence of anything to eat, would, he averred, be in no condition to face Dost Mahommed Khan until reinforcements should arrive; and the discussion having been continued in this strain until sunset, it terminated at length in his promising to make a forced march in the morning of double the distance, although nothing should induce either him or them to advance another step that night. Possessing no authority to act without the Affghans, or indeed to do more than second them if necessary, and Dost Mahommed Khan's escort being, moreover, unquestionably, too strong for our own small party, which consisted of no more than one hundred horse, I was compelled again to rest satisfied with the Khan's assurance, and most reluctantly to delay our advance.

All accounts agree in representing the fugitive to be escorted by at least two thousand followers, of whom nearly five hundred are said to be superior cavalry, whilst the rest consist of matchlock-men and Sussailchees; but their progress being retarded by the sickness of one of the young Princes, who is compelled to travel on a litter, our prospect of overtaking the party is greatly increased, and I have, therefore, distinctly informed Hadji Khan that, in the event of his hanging back on the morrow, we shall pursue the Ameer with our small detachment alone ; troubling him for none of the assistance which he appears so reluctantly to afford.

Shortly after nightfall Hadji Khan Kakur came over to my tent, and long endeavoured to impress upon me the rashness of our overtaking Dost Mahommed Khan, whose party so greatly exceeded our own in numerical strength; hinting that whilst many of our own Affghans were traitors, upon whom in the hour of need no dependance could be placed, the followers of the Ameer's fortunes were desperate, and bound in honour to sacrifice their lives in defence of their families, by whom they are accompanied. To this, I replied, that he was at liberty to act as he thought proper; but that, for our own parts, whenever we did come up with the fugitive, it was our determination to attack him, whether he assisted us or stayed behind. The waiting for a reinforcement, I informed him, was tantamount, he well knew, to giving Dost Mahommed Khan a free passport through the country, as it was not probable that the Ameer would await its arrival. Failing in his object of shaking our resolution, therefore, the Khan, at last, left the tent, and, seating himself a few yards from the door, conversed in the dark, in an undertone of voice, with three or four of his chiefs, for more than an hour. The latter were overheard to upbraid him for assisting the Feringees in their endeavours to arrest Dost Mahommed Khan, enquiring wherein the Ameer had ever injured him; and, although the result of their deliberations did not transpire, Hadji Khan was heard to admit the truth of all that they had advanced. It rained and hailed violently during the night, and our people have had nothing to eat for the last two days, except a little parched unripe corn.

CHAPTER XVI.

THE PURSUIT OF DOST MAHOMMED KHAN,— CONTINUED.

7th August. We marched at day-break, and, on arriving at Hurzar, found traces of the Ameer's encampment of yesterday. Perceiving these, Nuseerood-Dowlah stopped, on pretext of affording a little rest to his men, and was anxious to induce us to follow his example; but I insisted upon advancing at once with our own detachment. About a mile farther on the road, we were met by deserters from the camp of Dost Mahommed Khan, who informed us, that they had left the Ameer early this morning at Kalloo, and that there were then no signs of his being about to depart. I rode back instantly to Hadji Khan to apprize him of this piece of intelligence, entreating him to come on at once with his Affghans; but he again loudly protested against the madness of such a proceeding, declaring that we must inevitably be defeated, and thus bring disgrace upon the head of the Shah;—that by our precipitation we should drive the Ameer to desperation, whereas by his own *tudbeer* (precautions) he had closed the roads beyond Bamian, whence the fugitive could not possibly escape; and if we were but prudent, must assuredly fall into our hands. The Affghans, he added, were weary and hungry, and their immediate advance was therefore out of the question. Finding it impossible to overcome his scruples, I arose, and was proceeding to mount my horse, when Hadji Khan, following me, seized me by the arm, and loudly entreated me not to think of advancing, threatening rather to detain me by force, than to permit my rushing on certain destruction. Upon this I broke from him with the assurance that, although he might come on or tarry as he pleased, it was my full determination to march upon Kalloo, and, finding Dost Mahommed Khan there, to attack him, when, should I prove unsuccessful, *his* would be the disgrace, and *he* should answer for the consequences.

At 3 P. M. we reached Kalloo, only to have the mortification of finding, that Dost Mahommed Khan had departed so many hours previously, that he must, ere then, have surmounted the Kalloo Pass, the highest of the Hindoo Koosh. With horses and men knocked up, night fast approaching, and no signs of support from the Affghans, every one of whom had remained behind with the Khan at Hurzar, it was, of course, perfectly useless to proceed farther. We had already been nine hours in the saddle, and had crossed the Hajee Guk pass, twelve thousand feet above the ocean; the snow, from that height, being observable, lying at least fifteen hundred feet below us. When compared with the cross-paths, by which we had previously advanced, however, the road from

Yourt had proved excellent. In the evening we were so fortunate as to obtain a meal of flour for our men, encamping for the night at the foot of the Koh-i-Baba, literally 'the Father of mountains.' The summit of this peak, which has derived its name from the circumstance of its being the loftiest of the Hindoo-Koosh, is elevated twenty thousand feet above the level of the sea, and is covered with eternal snow.

On the morning of the 8th, we were joined by Captains Taylor and Trevor, with a reinforcement of thirty troopers, and about three hundred Affghans —whose presence appeared to have inspirited Nusseer-ood-Dowlah into coming up also; although he had not scrupled yesterday to leave us to face Dost Mahommed Khan by ourselves, and, equally unaided, to repel the *chuppao* or night attack, which he confidently predicted would be made on the part of the Ameer, and of which he himself entertained great alarm. Being ourselves, however, well aware that it was the sole object of the fugitive to escape, we had felt convinced that no attempt of an offensive nature would be made. Here Hadji Khan again urged upon me the necessity of our halting for further reinforcements, averring that Dost Mahommed Khan would undoubtedly make a determined stand at Bamian; beyond which place there was no prospect of his escaping, all the roads having been closed by the arrangements which he had made to raise the Huzarahs and other tribes. To this I again replied as before, that it was only by overtaking Dost Mahommed Khan at Bamian, that we could feel at all assured of his making a stand there; whereas by delaying, we, in my opinion, rendered the escape of the fugitive certain, my reliance on his (Hadji Khan's) tudbeer, being, at best, very slender.

He then went over the old ground, and reiterated the certainty of our being defeated, to the tarnishing of the Shah's fame; but I informed him, that there was in our dictionary no such word as *retreat*, and that we did not choose, under any circumstances, to risk our own fame by suffering Dost Mahommed Khan to effect his escape unmolested, so long as there existed the most remote prospect of our being able to overtake him—concluding by assuring him, that the disgrace would fall upon those who hung back from the encounter, and would in no degree attach itself to us, so long as we strove, at all hazards, to effect the object upon which we had been dispatched by the Shah. On my proceeding to mount my horse, the Khan again laid hold of me, and after endeavouring by entreaties to detain me, had recourse, as before, to menaces of force, which ended in his actually withholding the guides. Breaking from him, however, and marching on my men without them, I was soon afterwards agreeably surprised at perceiving the Hadji also advancing,—a step to which he had, I presume, been forced by very shame.

In the course of this day we surmounted the pass of Shutur-i-gardan, or the Camel's neck, of which the altitude is not given by Sir Alexander Burnes, who, finding it impassable from snow in the month of May, was obliged to adopt a more circuitous route. We estimated the height to be at least three thousand feet above the pass of Hajee Guk, over which we had travelled yesterday; the acclivity being so extremely steep, that we were compelled to lead our horses the whole way up; and the descent, although less abrupt, being even greater than the ascent.

Arriving after dark, at a deserted village at the foot of the ghaut, we halted on the banks of a stream which flows into the Oxus, less with a view of resting our fatigued horses, than to admit of the Affghans coming up. On learning from me my intention of pressing on to Bamian at 2 o'clock in the morning, Nusseer-ood-Dowlah implored me not to think of advancing until dawn, few of his own people having yet arrived, and there existing, in his opinion, no probability whatever of Dost Mahommed Khan's escaping beyond that place. At length, finding that all other arguments failed in shaking my determination, he plainly informed me that he was so surrounded by traitors amongst the Affghans, that he could not venture to march with them at night. "In broad daylight," he continued, "I may be able to take them on, but if you do encounter Dost Mahommed Khan, not one of the Affghans will draw a sword against him, nor will I be responsible that they do not turn against yourself in the *melee*." On my return he insisted upon sending a guard with me, having previously stated, that it was not safe that I should proceed unattended amongst the Affghans, so far even as my own bivouac.

This refusal, on the part of Hadji Khan Kakur, added to the fact of our horses being completely knocked up by the day's work, compelled us to wait patiently until daybreak, sending on, however, two officers of our party to reconnoitre, with instructions to gallop back from Bamian with information of any symptoms that might be observed of the intended departure thence of Dost Mahommed Khan, in order that we might, in that case, hasten our advance accordingly. In the mean time a council of war having been held, it was resolved that on the Ameer turning to oppose us, of which, on our overtaking him to-morrow, as we expect to do, there can be no doubt, the thirteen British officers, who are present with this force, shall charge in the centre of the little band, every one directing his individual efforts against the person of Dost Mahommed Khan, whose fall must thus be rendered next to certain. It being evident that all the Affghans on both sides will turn against us, unless we are immediately successful, this plan of attack appears to afford the only chance of escape to those who may survive; and it is an object of paramount importance to effect the destruction of the Ameer, rather than to permit his escape. Although crowded as usual into one small rowtie, (marquee,) with little to eat, nothing whatever to drink, and no bed on which to lie, saving our sheep-skin cloaks, our little party, always cheerful and merry, has never been more happy than on this night, under the exciting expectation of so glorious a struggle in the morning. All prospect of danger on such occasions as these is met by the soldier with the gratifying conviction that should he fall, he will have earned an enviable place in the recollection of those loved, though distant friends, in whose memory he most desires to live.

CHAPTER XVII.

THE ESCAPE OF DOST MAHOMMED KHAN.

9th August. Whilst in the act of mounting our horses, at break of day, information was brought in that Dost Mahommed Khan, instead of halting yesterday at Bamian, as, from the reiterated assurances of Hadji Khan, we had been led to anticipate, had, on the contrary, passed through that place in the forenoon; and his family having previously been sent on, had himself pushed forward at once to Akrabad, another march in advance. This morning he was to be at Sygan, twenty-five or thirty miles farther, on the verge of the Shah's territory; and, to-night, at Kamurdunda, under the protection of the "Waly," an independent Uzbek Chieftain, who is at enmity with Shah Shooja ool Moolk. Upon receiving this intelligence, I informed Nusseer-ood-Dowlah, that, should it prove to be correct, he should answer with his head for the escape of the Ameer Dost Mahommed Khan.

Arriving at Bamian, twelve miles in advance, we there found about seventy horsemen, who had shortly before been dismissed by the Ameer; and they, as well as two spies belonging to the mission, whom we also found, confirm the information received this morning, together with all that had previously been reported to us respecting the strength of his escort. They also state, that the young Prince is now sufficiently recovered to be able to exchange the litter, in which he has hitherto travelled, for the back of an elephant. There being, under such circumstances, not the smallest hope of our now overtaking the fugitive within the Shah's territories, to which we have been restricted, or indeed of inducing the Affghans to advance one step farther,—the officers of our Cavalry having, moreover, represented that their horses are incapable, through want of food and rest, of making further forced marches immediately, we have here been compelled to relinquish the pursuit, nothing being now left for us but to await the result of a letter which I yesterday forwarded through Hadji Khan Kakur to the Chiefs who accompany the Ameer. Here we have obtained both green corn and peas for our people, and, although no grain is to be had, there is abundance of good forage for the horses.

10th. Early this morning, a message from Nusseer-ood-Dowlah requested my attendance at a meeting, already convened, of all the Affghan Sirdars. Accompanied by Lieutenant Hogg I repaired thither immediately, and found him, along with about twenty of the Chiefs, seated in an open field, and surrounded by a mob of followers, who, on our approach, met me with clamorous demands to return,—Hadji Khan himself taking the lead, and declaring roundly that, having no food for his people, neither he nor they would stay a minute longer. I replied, that my people were as badly off as his, but that they were content to subsist upon parched corn, in preference to giving up the service upon which they had been sent out; that it behoved none of us to go back until we had received the Shah's orders, or, at all events, until sufficient time had been allowed for an answer to arrive to the letter which had been addressed yesterday to the adherents of Dost Mahommed Khan. Nusseer-ood-Dowlah continuing obstinate, I informed him, that he might go or stay as he pleased, but that we should remain where we were, and should make him answer to the King for any consequences to ourselves from his desertion.

I then returned to my own tent, whither both Hadji Khan and the Chiefs shortly followed me; the latter, in order to beg that I would reconsider my rash resolve, and depart at once. "We have arrived," they said, "thus far without molestation, through the protection of the Khan alone; and, once deprived of it, cannot fail to be destroyed by the surrounding tribes, which are now only restrained by their awe of his presence." To all this, however, I did but repeat my determination not to move until, at least, time had been given for the arrival of an answer to our letter; whereupon the Khan immediately applied for a written paper, authorising his own departure. This I, of course, refused, assuring him, at the same time, that his going would be his own act and deed, and none of my bidding. Then, turning to two of the principal Chiefs, whom I knew

to be independent of Hadji Khan, I stated distinctly
to them, that, although I cared not whether the Khan
went or stayed, I should, nevertheless, expect them
to remain. From an apprehension of offending Nusseer-ood-Dowlah, I conclude, they returned no
answer at the time, although they afterwards sent
to promise adherence to us. Hadji Khan, on rising
to retire, exclaimed, " Well, I shall wait until
to-morrow morning;" and then, taking off his turban, he added, "and I call upon you all to witness
that, bare-headed, I have entreated the Sahib to
return; the consequences of his not accompanying
me to-morrow are, therefore, now on his own head."
Information was brought to us, in the evening, that
Hadji Khan's people had been overheard remarking
amongst themselves that they, as well as the inhabitants of the country, had been ordered to do us all
the injury in their power, after the departure of the
Khan in the morning.

11th. The Chiefs, who had promised adherence
to us, came betimes to complain that, on learning of
their resolution last night, Hadji Khan had severely
abused them; but, failing to shake their resolution,
had himself been ultimately obliged to relinquish
his intention of leaving. Horses were, nevertheless,
saddled, and every preparation having been made
by the Khan for departure, he sent to request an
interview. I returned for answer that he was already in possession of my sentiments, and that, as
they were unchangeable, further communication was
useless. He came over, in spite of this, and, with
the deepest hypocrisy, declared that, although most

of his followers had deserted, he had himself determined not to leave us, and would stand by us to the last. I replied that, although I should not have regretted his departure, it was, perhaps, well for himself that he had altered his mind; adding, that I now suspected he had never forwarded any letter whatever to the adherents of Dost Mahommed Khan, inasmuch as four days were amply sufficient to have put us in possession of a reply; and I concluded, by informing him that, unless an answer should be received by noon on the following day, it was my intention to return to the Shah, having received from himself no assistance whatever towards provisioning my men, notwithstanding that I was well informed of his having levied from the district, on his own account, one hundred sheep, and seven kurwars of grain. I then addressed to the Envoy and Minister the following letter:—

'Bamian, 11th August, 1839.

'SIR,—On my arrival at this place, on the 9th instant, I had the honor to address you, with information that the Ameer Dost Mahommed Khan had escaped beyond the frontier; expressing, at the same time, my intention to await the result of a letter, that had been addressed to his adherents by Nusseer-ood-Dowlah, myself, and others, or the receipt of further orders from yourself.

'The accompanying extracts from my journal will explain to you the circumstances under which I have been compelled to resolve on returning from Bamian to-morrow, at midday, unless supplies, reinforcements, or orders to the contrary, shall be received by that time; when, having completed three days at this place, a sufficient period will have elapsed to admit of an answer arriving from the adherents of Dost Mahommed Khan to the letter addressed to them on the 8th instant, if it ever was really despatched by Hadji Khan Kakur, which I have now reason to doubt.

'You will regret to observe that the conduct of Nusseer-ood-Dowlah, if not criminal, has been most blameable, throughout; his backwardness having favoured the escape of the Ameer Dost Mahommed Khan, whose capture was inevitable, had the Khan pushed on, as he might have done, as I repeatedly urged him to do, and as his troops were perfectly capable of doing.

'It will be seen, from the diary, that the fugitive might have been overtaken at Hurzar on the morning of the 6th instant, had not our guides, who were under charge of Nusseer-ood-Dowlah's people, deserted us during the night; that the Khan then insisted on delaying at Yourt, only half-way to Hurzar, instead of pushing on, as urged by me to do; and that, although he promised to make up for the delay in the afternoon, he ultimately refused to go on; thus retarding our advance till next morning, the 7th instant, when we expected to overtake Dost Mahommed Khan at Kulloo, to which place, in that hope, I was compelled to proceed with the British detachment alone, unsupported by Nusseer-ood-

Dowlah, or any of the Affghan troops, who remained behind, at Hurzar, nowithstanding my personal solicitations to that Chief.

'It will be further seen that he, next day, again endeavoured to prevent our following the fugitive; that he deceived me, by repeated false assurances of Dost Mahommed Khan's escape being cut off; and, finally, that he formally announced to me his inability to face Dost Mahommed Khan with his own Affghans, not a man of whom, he declared, would fight against the Ameer; even hinting his belief that they were more likely to turn against ourselves.

'The whole of the proceedings of Nusséer-ood-Dowlah have thus displayed either the grossest cowardice, or the deepest treachery; and I have now performed my duty in making them known to you.

'I have the honor to be, &c.'

12th. Retraced our steps, at midday, twelve miles, to the village situated at the foot of the Kalloo pass, our route following the channel of a stream which falls into the Oxus.—13th. Marched again, at daybreak, the ascent of the pass occupying two-and-a-half, and the descent one-and-a-half hours. Halted at the foot of the Hajee Guk pass, after being in the saddle five-and-a-quarter hours; the distance we estimated to be twelve miles. Hadji Khan Kakur urges our marching to-morrow to Oomje, seven or eight miles beyond Yourt, this being, at least, seventeen miles farther than we could induce him to march during our advance, when expedition was so great an object, and while our horses were far more fresh than they now are. On that occasion, no entreaties could prevail on him to come on from Yourt to our present ground, where Dost Mahommed Khan was then supposed to be ; but, having himself halted with his Affghans nine miles short of this place, he suffered us to proceed by ourselves, to encounter the Ameer.

14th August. During last night, the water in our wash-hand basons was frozen over. Marched to within a short distance of Gurdan dewal, over a good horse-road. An easy ascent, of about half-a-mile, leads to the top of the Hajee Guk pass, on the summit of which we found the pools frozen. Thence, the path descends down the bed of a stream, the whole way to the Helmont river, on which Gurdan dewal is situated. We were five-and-a-half hours in the saddle, and estimated the distance at eighteen or nineteen miles.

15th. To Sir-i-Chushma, nominally the source of the Cabul river, but we had in reality followed a rivulet for ten miles, before reaching these copious streams which here unite with it. Five hours in the saddle. Estimated distance seventeen or eighteen miles, the first five or six leading over numerous steep stony ascents and declivities to the summit of a pass, the name of which has escaped me—and thence descending the whole way through a narrow valley.—16th. Kot-i-Ashroo. Five hours, seventeen miles ; the road being a continuation of the same valley, which widens and terminates at Meidan.—17th. Over the Oomjee pass to Cabul, six hours. The path easy, and not very steep, and the estimated distance twenty miles.

19th. Nusseer-ood-Dowlah arrested, by order of the King, on charge of treason, and for having favoured the escape of Dost Mahommed Khan:— undeniable proofs against him having now been obtained, in addition to the palpable obstacles which he threw in the way of our pursuit of the fugitive, and his personal refusal to advance, when the Ameer was known to be within our reach.

I here take leave of Hadji Khan Kakur, but the reader will find his early history in a paper, by Mr. Masson, in the Transactions of the Bombay Geographical Society, for May last.

From what I personally gathered, it appears that he commenced life in the humble capacity of a melon vender, and raised himself to the highest rank, by cunning and enterprise, though, strange to say, invariably changing sides, when his interest prompted him to do so. Having deserted Dost Mahommed Khan, to join the Candahar Sirdars, he abandoned the latter, on our approach to that city, thus forcing them to fly, without striking a blow. For this service, Shah Shooja ennobled him, by the title of Nusseer-ood-Dowlah, and conferred on him a jaghire of three lacs of rupees annually, in the vain hope of purchasing his fidelity; but it has now transpired that he had actually leagued himself with others to attack the King, on any change of fortune; and, with this view, had stood aloof with his Affghans, until the day after Ghizni fell, when he presented himself, with the most lavish professions of devotion.

Again, he was entrusted with the pursuit of Dost Mahommed Khan, it being naturally supposed that he was too deeply committed against that Chief, to admit of a possibility of their coalition; but he was, nevertheless, engaged in a correspondence with him during the whole proceeding, and the result has been shown in the foregoing pages. It is now only necessary to add, that he is a State prisoner, at Chunar.

CHAPTER XVIII.

OPERATIONS AGAINST THE GHILJEES.

On the 21st of August I was temporarily placed at the disposal of the Envoy and Minister with his Majesty Shah Shooja ul Mulk, for the purpose of conducting an expedition into certain disturbed districts lying between Cabul and Candahar, in order to tranquillize the disaffected Ghiljee tribes, none of whom had yet submitted to the King. The undertaking was, however, of necessity postponed until the arrival from Candahar of the treasure convoy, expected about the end of the month; and in the meantime I remained unoccupied at Cabul.

25th. Received from the Envoy my instructions relative to the approaching expedition. They are dated this day, and are to the following effect, viz.: to depose, and if possible to arrest the refractory Ghiljee Chiefs, Mehta Moossa Khan, Abdool Rehman Khan, Gool Mahommed Khan, and the Mama;* and to establish the newly-appointed Ghiljee Governors, Meer Allum Khan, Zeman Khan, and Khulleel Khan; to punish the inhabitants of Maroof, who, in

* So called from the circumstance of his being the uncle of the Sirdars of Candahar.

May last, wantonly destroyed a caravan proceeding from Hindostan to Candahar;—and, lastly, to reduce the forts of Nusseer-ood-Dowlah, should they still be held by his adherents.

The cold-blooded murder of Colonel Herring having been yesterday reported, I have further been directed also to punish the perpetrators of that atrocity, and my departure in advance will be hastened in consequence.

The detachment placed under my orders is composed of a wing of the Shah's 1st Cavalry and Goorkah Battalion, and Captain Abbott's Battery of 9-prs. from Cabul; which are to be reinforced from Candahar by Captain Macan's Regiment of the Shah's Infantry, half of the Shah's 2d Regiment of Cavalry, and a Brigade of Horse Artillery. One thousand Affghan Cavalry were also to have accompanied me from hence, but in consideration of the difficulty that would be experienced in foraging so large a force, as well as in restraining them from plunder, the number has been reduced at my own request to five hundred. These, divided into small parties varying in strength, are led respectively by twenty Affghan Chiefs;—the whole under the command of Mahommed Oosman Khan, a nobleman of great consideration, and uncle to the King.

5th September. His Majesty received me according to previous appointment in open durbar, where he introduced the Affghan Chiefs who are to accompany me against the Ghiljees. After addressing them at considerable length, requiring them to afford me implicit obedience, and warning them of the fate of Nusseer-ood-Dowlah, should they fail in the proper discharge of their duty, His Majesty accompanied by Captain Macgregor, Assistant to the Envoy and Minister, and myself, withdrew to his private apartment, where, for upwards of an hour, he conversed, chiefly on the subject of my approaching expedition. On my return from the palace, I was met by the Affghan Chiefs, who importuned me for leave to put off their departure for three days. On this score I referred them to the King, informing them distinctly, at the same time, that whether they were prepared or not, I should myself march the following day with the Hindostanee Cavalry under Captain Nicolson, leaving the Artillery and Infantry to proceed, when ready, direct to Ghizni.

7th. Marched at sun-rise from Cabul to Chariser, six-and-a-half miles on the Loghur road. Only three hundred of the Shah's Hindostanee Cavalry, and one hundred of Skinner's Horse, accompanied me; but I received from the King a promise that he would *drive* the Affghans after me in the course of the day.—8th. None of the Affghans arrived. Continued my route through an open valley, and over a good road, fifteen miles, to Mahommed Aga, on the Loghur river. Heavy rain fell.—9th. Halted to admit of the Affghans coming up, but not one of them appeared. Sirwa Khan, the Lohanee Chief, whose services I had secured, joined me in the afternoon. Rain in the evening, and a heavy fall again during the night.

10th. Baboos, eleven miles. A letter from the Envoy informs me, that the King and himself have at length succeeded in driving after me the Affghans, who are all now on the road—Mr. Macnaghten also acquaints me, that certain hostile indications, on the part of the Ameer Dost Mahommed Khan, having rendered necessary the dispatch to Bamian of the Goorkah Battalion, a wing of the 16th Regiment Bengal Native Infantry, now at Ghizni, has been placed at my disposal in lieu thereof.—11th. Mulkabad, thirteen-and-a-half miles,—none of the Affghans have yet joined.—12th. Marched nineteen-and-a-quarter miles, to Alli Jah's Killa, in the Khurvar district. At the twelfth mile we reached the foot of the Khurvar pass, the ascent by which is three quarters of a mile in length, extremely steep and difficult—and infinitely worse than that of the Kojak. Having been detained until 4 p. m. in assisting the baggage camels over, I left one hundred horse to bring up those of the commissariate, pushing forward myself with the rest of the party to this place—my object being the apprehension of the Chief, Buxee Khan, whom, I have ascertained to be in close connexion with the body of marauders that murdered Colonel Herring. We found that the Chief had unfortunately gone off some time before with his family, but we succeeded in arresting several of his nearest male relatives, and in taking possession of all his forts, five in number. Whilst occupied at the pass, I was joined by Meer Allum Khan, one of the Ghiljee Governors whom I am to instal. He reports that the Affghan Cavalry will be here to-morrow.

13th. Mahommed Oosman Khan and his Affghans have arrived at the village on this side of the Khurwar pass; but they have sent to request my

permission to their remaining behind until to-morrow, in order to assist in bringing over their baggage, which is still on the other side of the hills.—
14th. The Affghans joined. Despatched a body of sixty horsemen, under the command of Meer Allum Khan, for the purpose of apprehending a branch party of the gang that murdered Colonel Herring; which is said to be in the neighbourhood of Churka. Late at night received Meer Allum Khan's report that he had succeeded in securing six of this banditti.—15th and 16th. Occupied in making over the forts and property of Buxee Khan to the neighbouring Zemindars,—receiving their engagements to maintain and answer for the same to the Shah.

17th. After despatching our nine prisoners to Ghizni, marched at day-break for the Zoormul valley, with two hundred and fifty Hindostanee Cavalry, composed of the Shah's and Skinner's Horse, together with four hundred Affghan horse; leaving the remainder of my detachment to preserve the tranquillity of Khurwar until the capture of Buxee Khan. The Affghan allies are in great alarm at the idea of penetrating into the Zoormul valley, wherein some doughty Douranee chieftain was formerly defeated and slain;—none of the kings of the country having, they aver, ever ventured to enter it, unless at the head of a large army, owing to the number and daring of the tribes in that quarter, said to amount to some thousands. We passed two ranges of hills, and at 1 p. m., after a march of seventeen miles, arrived at the fort of Futteh Ooll' Khan. Much commotion had been observed in th many neighbouring forts with which the valley is studded, as far as the eye can reach; but I despatched emissaries for the purpose of re-assuring the people, and before evening a free and friendly intercourse had been established. On first entering the valley, I despatched a party of horse, under Meer Allum Khan, to ascertain whether Buxee Khan had not found refuge in a Fort belonging to a relation, and lying some miles higher up; in which case I directed him to invest the place, and send me notice immediately .Meer Allum Khan returned, however, in the evening, and reported that although the fugitive was in the fort in question so late as last night, he had fled this very morning with all his relatives, and had left the place empty.

18th. Joined by a wing of the 16th Regiment Bengal Native Infantry, under the command of Major McLaren. Several of the principal families in the Zoormul and Gurdaiz districts tendered their allegiance to the Shah; and it was ascertained from the leading men, who attended for this purpose, that four days prior to our arrival, a circular letter had been addressed to them all by Mehta Moossa Khan, the Ghiljee Chief, calling upon them to rise *en masse*, and to occupy the intermediate passes, in order that they might oppose my entrance into the valley. They had, however, refused to commit themselves by any such act of hostility, being, they said, well aware that our armies exercise no oppression, and pursue none but the guilty.

20th. Received accounts of the capture of Buxee Khan by the detachment left for that purpose at

Khurwar.—21st. Made a night march, in order to surprise the Kanjuk banditti, whose haunt I had ascertained to be in the Indran mountains, eighteen miles to the eastward. Arrived, as the day broke, at a deep dell occupied by the gang; and while the Infantry advanced from the front, I despatched the horse, in two bodies, to cut off retreat from flanks and rear. The ground being very broken and difficult, however, most of the enemy had found time to ascend a precipitous hill, along the ridge of which they must have escaped, had I not fortunately been mounted on an exceedingly active horse, and thus been enabled to gallop ahead, and deter them from advancing until the Cavalry came up. Finding themselves completely surrounded, they defended themselves most stoutly; and maintained their position until their ammunition was nearly all expended, when on a general rush being made from every quarter at once, they were induced to throw down their arms, after sixteen of the most desperate of their body had been killed, and several others wounded. Even the women assisted in the fray, by handing ammunition to their husbands, and throwing stones at our troops. The loss on our side amounts to three sepoys and one horse killed, and two Lieutenants, one Rissaldar, and one Duffedar, and several men and horses wounded. In the evening we returned with one hundred and twelve prisoners, comprising some women and children, who, with the men killed in the attack, form the whole of the Kanjuk gang then present. Not a soul contrived to escape, and the whole of their arms and property, together with a hundred and twelve camels, have fallen into our hands—nearly all the latter bearing the Company's mark, shewing that they were stolen from the British army during its advance.

23d. Selected forty-six of the most desperate of the prisoners for transmission to Cabul; where they will, in all probability, be executed, in presence of the troops for the murder of Colonel Herring.—25th. Marched to Shore Kutch, fifteen miles.—26th. Advanced to Chulluk, six miles.—28th. To Mooshkail, fourteen miles, where Mehta Moossa Khan, one of the refractory Ghiljee Chiefs, and leader of the fanatic army, which threatened the British camp the day before the fall of Ghizni, came in and surrendered. On the 29th, marched eighteen miles to Malinda, and on the 30th, fifteen more to Punna.

CHAPTER XIX.

OPERATIONS AGAINST THE GHILJEES,—CONTINUED.

1st October. Marched to Okori, fourteen miles, and directed the detachment of the Shah's 1st Cavalry, under Lieutenant Nicolson, to return to Cabul; all the horses being completely knocked up, from hard work and want of forage.—2d. To Ooshlan, fourteen miles, where we halted on the 3rd, and were joined, from the camp of General Willshire, (which is three marches on our right,) by the Poona Auxiliary Horse, under Captain Keith Erskine.—4th. Advanced to Deelah, thirteen-and-a-quarter miles, situated on the great salt lake mentioned by Sooltan Baber, and of which I estimate the diameter to be about twelve miles: on the banks of the Ghizni stream, which here flows into it, thousands of dead fish were strewed. Marched in the evening, seventeen-and-a-half miles, to Munsoor, where, on our arrival about midnight, we found our three 9-pr guns, escorted by a wing of the 19th Regiment Bombay Native Infantry, from Ghizui, awaiting us, according to previous appointment.

5th. Pushed on to Feroze, twelve miles, making a total of forty-two-and-a-half miles in twenty-four hours.—6th. Reached Killa-i-Murgha, the fort of Abdool Rehman Khan, the principal Ghiljee Chief, whose father, when disputing empire with Shah Zeman, besieged Cabul with fifty thousand horse and foot; and the same who himself kept our army so much on the alert during its march from Candahar to Ghizni. Surprised the Chief in his stronghold; a well-constructed fort, possessing a high citadel and a wet ditch. It had twice been besieged, unsuccessfully, by Shah Shooja ool Moolk, during his former temporary reign. Abdool Rehman Khan had, however, intended to fly on the present occasion; and, prior to our sudden arrival, had sent off the whole of his women and property, retaining with him eighty select horsemen only. It was my object to defer taking this place until the following evening, by which time the Cavalry would be sufficiently rested, to enable me to make a dash at the other rebel chiefs, (the Mama and Goroo), whose forts are situated within a forced march of Killa-i-Murgha, while those chiefs supposed us still occupied with Abdool Rehman, whom they might reasonably have expected to keep us at bay for some time. I therefore requested Major McLaren to content himself with merely watching the fort, and in the evening that officer took measures to prevent escape during the night, by surrounding it with upwards of five hundred Cavalry, and posting two Companies of the 16th Regiment Bengal Native Infantry under cover, within two hundred yards of the gate; with orders to form and move up on any appearance of the coming out of the garrison.

At sun-set the enemy opened a fire from the walls on our videttes; by which Lieutenant Jeffery, 19th Regiment, was wounded; and this was continued until 11 P. M. without a shot being returned. They then suddenly dashed on horseback past our picquets, and unfortunately no warning having been given in the manner intended, for the Cavalry to close in, the enemy were unchecked in their rush, and dispersed in every direction, followed by the videttes, who mixed with the fugitives. Owing to the extreme darkness, the picquets were unable to distinguish friend from foe, and thus every man escaped. On the alarm being given, I gallopped after with such few horsemen as I happened to meet, and followed in the direction the fugitives were said to have taken; but, in consequence of the total darkness, the pursuit proved to no purpose. It was afterwards ascertained that three of the wives of Abdool Rehman Khan, and his sister, who is one of the wives of Dost Mahommed Khan, had ridden off with him. He had expected to be joined by a neighbouring Chief, the Khan of the Teerkies, who being secretly in my interests, had promised to raise his 'ooloos' (tribe) and come to his aid; and in this confidence Abdool Rehman Khan had remained until evening in the manner described; intending to make a sortie, when the Khan with his clan, reported to be some thousand strong, should approach to attack our camp in the rear. But this illusion was dispelled by the setting sun, when the rebel chief had the mortification of perceiving his pretended ally march into our camp as a friend!

During the 7th and 8th we were occupied upon the demolition of the fort, which was completely destroyed by mines carried under the citadel, towers and gateway. On the evening of the 8th I rode to the camp of General Willshire at Hyderkail, twenty miles; and, although escorted by two common Ghiljee followers only, I was suffered to pass unmolested through several villages inhabited by various Ghiljee tribes. This is one convincing proof how completely this turbulent class has been quelled; and we have also lately experienced the results of the wholesome chastisement, which it has been found necessary to inflict, in the fact of our cattle being permitted to graze, and our people to go about, at a distance from the camp, beyond the precincts of which, during the advance of the army, the first would inevitably have been carried off, and the latter as surely murdered. It being late at night when I reached the British camp, and most of the officers having gone to bed, I knocked up the Staff to request a halt to-morrow, in order to enable me to act from hence against the Mama, in case he should be in occupation of his fort. The flight of Abdool Rehman Khan has rendered this less probable, but I still entertain hopes that certain emissaries of mine, who are now with the Mama, may succeed in inducing him to hold out.

9th. The necessary information, not having yet been brought, no movement has been made. A detachment, consisting of a wing of H. M.'s 17th Foot,

Captain Lloyd's Battery, the Poona Auxiliary Horse, and a squadron of the 1st Light Cavalry, has been told off by General Willshire to remain with me, for the performance of any service that may be found necessary, whilst the main body of his division continues its march.—11th. Joined by the detachment under Major McLaren. Intelligence having now been received that the Mama and Gooroo had fled immediately upon learning of the escape of Abdool Rehman Khan, this day was occupied in concerting measures for the eventual capture of the fugitives. This I hope to accomplish through the agency of the hill tribe of Nasseries, (with whose chief I have established a good understanding,) who occupy the country through which the rebels must pass on their way to the Punjab, whither it is said they purpose taking refuge. I have also despatched to the Seik authorities, at Dera-i-Ismael Khan, a message, soliciting their co-operation with the Nasserie Chief, should he stand in need of assistance, and requesting them also to receive charge of the prisoners, if captured.* Directed the return to Ghizni of Major McLaren's detachment, and of the Shah's Affghans to Cabul, viâ Mokoor, in order to apprehend certain persons residing at the latter place, who stand accused of the murder of Lieutenant Inverarity at Candahar in May last. In the evening I rode to General Willshire's camp, Khan Teerkee, ten miles, whither my detachment had marched in the morning to rejoin.

12th. Marched with the Bombay Column to

* I have not yet learned the result of these measures.

Kistni, twelve miles.—13th. Crossed the Goodan pass to Goondan, eleven miles.—14th. Halted.—16th. Sewa, nine-and-three-quarter miles.—15th. Sperioury, eleven-and-three-quarter miles.—17th. Left the camp at 1 A. M. with a squadron of H. M.'s 4th Light Dragoons, the Poona Auxiliary Horse, four 24-pr. howitzers, a detachment of Sappers and Miners, and a wing of the 19th Regiment Bombay Native Infantry, the whole under the command of Lieutenant Colonel Stalker, on an expedition against the Barukzye tribes of Maroof, who had plundered, and cruelly treated, the Hindostanee kafila, which left Candahar in May last. Arriving at daybreak within sight of the principal Barukzye villages, I gallopped on with the Cavalry, and surrounded them before a soul had time to escape. Aboo Khan and Jubbar Khan, the Chiefs of the tribe, together with all their followers, were thus secured; and they informed against others concerned, whom I also apprehended, by proceeding immediately to their villages with a few horsemen. Having placed the prisoners in charge of the Infantry, I crossed the valley to the fort of Maroof, which, in consequence of the approach of the Bombay Column, had been evacuated some days before. To my astonishment, it proved to be the strongest fortress that we had yet seen in the country, being constructed with *double* gates, a ditch, faussebraye, and towers of solid masonry, which might have held out successfully against all the *materiel* with which the Bombay Division is provided.

18th. Sent back the Artillery and Dragoons, and remained with the Sappers and 19th Regiment, in order to destroy the fort, which before nightfall had been effectually accomplished, by blowing up the gateway and principal towers.—19th. Forwarded to Candahar, under charge of Captain Walker, commanding the detachment of the Shah's 2d Cavalry, nine prisoners selected for example, and released the remainder. Directed the return of Captain Macan's detachment, which had marched from Candahar to Kelat-i-Ghiljee to join me, but which I had not occasion to employ. None of the Shah's troops now remain with me. General Willshire's Division having advanced two marches since we left it, I rejoined his camp at Sir-i-Soorakah, by a march of twenty miles, across a range of mountains.

20th. Marched with the Bombay Column, fourteen miles.—21st. Eight miles.—22d. Gokaruk, twelve miles.—23d. Halted. The road for the last three days has lain through a succession of mountains, which, from their fantastic figures, might be likened to the ocean, petrified during a storm. Excepting an occasional shepherd's tent, no human habitation has been observed the whole way.—24th. Oker Sahib, twelve miles.—25th. Near to Toba, one of the forts of Hadji Khan Kakur, eight miles. The garrison of this place having fired upon our foragers, I proceeded with two guns and two companies of Europeans, intending to blow open and storm the gate; but on our arrival we found it totally deserted. The greater part of the garrison had fled with all their property some days before, leaving behind a few matchlock-men only, who, before we could come up, had also absconded. The place was too paltry to require that it should be destroyed.

26th. To Shah Gullee, thirteen miles.—27th. Badshara, nine miles.—28th. Soorkar, eighteen miles, emerging about mid-way of this march from the hills over and through which we have been labouring for the last fortnight. At the gorge of the pass stands a large fort of Hadji Khan Kakur's, to reconnoitre which, I preceded the column, intending, should it prove to be occupied, to take it as soon as the troops came up. Finding it evacuated, we passed on, but having heard in the course of the day that a body of Hadji Khan's mounted followers had threatened our baggage, and cut down two of our followers, I resolved to turn and destroy their stronghold. For this purpose General Willshire left with me the Sappers and Miners, and two companies of Europeans, together with two guns, and a squadron of Dragoons, to support if necessary.

29th. Retraced my steps, eight miles, with the above detachment, to Hadji Khan's fort; and having completely demolished it, by blowing up every bastion, gateway, and outwork, returned again in the evening. By the inhabitants of this extensive valley, the destruction of this fortress is hailed with the greatest joy; commanding, as it did, the stream which supplies their villages, its garrison could stop or turn off the water at pleasure—thus holding all at their mercy; and since the arrest of their Chief at Cabul, they have exercised a regular system of aggression upon their defenceless neighbours.—30th.

Made a double march of twenty-five miles, to overtake General Willshire at Koochlak; and on the 31st, advanced eleven miles more, with the Bombay Column, to Quetta.

CHAPTER XX.

ADVANCE UPON KHELAT.

Leaving the whole of the Cavalry, and nearly all of the Artillery of the Bombay Column, together with the Park and the 19th Regiment Bombay Native Infantry to proceed down the Bolan pass, Major General Willshire marched on the 4th of November from Quetta upon Khelat, taking only H. M.'s 2d and 17th Foot, and the 31st Bengal Native Infantry, the ranks of all three mustering very weak;—six light field pieces, consisting of two guns of the Bombay Horse Artillery, and four of the Shah's;—the Engineer Corps, and one hundred and fifty Irregular Horse,—the whole in the highest possible order. This arrangement had been rendered necessary in consequence of the deficiency that was represented to exist on the road in respect to water and forage; and General Willshire has been the less reluctant to dispense with so large a portion of his Division, from the expected submission of Mehrab Khan, the Chief of Khelat. I have mislaid our journal of our first seven marches, with one halt, viâ Mustung, but no incident worth relating occurred during that period.

The road was excellent, and quite contrary to the expectations we had been led to form ; both water and forage proved to be so abundant, that the whole of the division might have marched without the smallest difficulty.

11th. We are now two moderate marches from Khelat, and the tone assumed by Mehrab Khan is any thing but humble. A letter this day received from him, falls indeed little short of defiance. It directs the immediate halt of the British troops, pending his negociations,—and warns them to take the consequences of an advance to the intermediate stage, to which he avows his intention of moving out to-day with his whole army. Although our sources of information are not much to be depended upon, we have every reason to believe that Mehrab Khan has actually assembled at his capital, upwards of two thousand of the *élite* of the warriors of Belochistan; and we know the Wullee Mahommed Khan, the Chief of Wudd and of the Menghul tribe of Beloches, who is styled 'Leader of eighteen thousand,' is with him, together with many others of the principal Beloche Chieftains; and, moreover, that his son is daily expected to arrive with strong reinforcements from Noshky. Our own force is therefore sufficiently small; but we have, of course, no misgivings as to the result. Should the chief meet us in the field tomorrow, as he threatens to do, our success will probably be immediate and complete. If he wait for us behind the walls of Khelat, we may have greater difficulties to overcome ; but in event of our failing to carry the place by a *coup de main*, there can be no doubt of our being eventually able to effect an entrance by mining. After the example so recently made of Ghizni, we must naturally expect to find the gates blocked up, and perhaps rendered altogether impracticable, but we may yet have an opportunity of demonstrating to the people of this country, that there are other roads of access to a fort than by a gateway; and we know that there is no ditch around Khelat, and that the walls, which are composed of mud, are not very high.

My political functions having ceased on entering the valley of Shawl, (Quetta) which, together with Khelat, is under the charge of Captain Bean, I have accompanied the troops hither as an amateur, but General Willshire has kindly nominated me to attend him in capacity of Aide-de-Camp during the expected action; and with the sanction of Captain Peat, the Chief Engineer, has consented to my serving with the Engineers during the siege.

12th. Accompanied by Lieut. John Ramsay, Assistant Quarter Master General, and escorted by twenty Local Horse, I was despatched in advance of the troops, to reconnoitre the enemy's position, in event of his having fulfilled his threat of moving out to the ground we intend occupying to-day. We were met about half way by some mounted scouts, who gallopped off the moment they saw us; and about three miles from our proposed ground, we observed a small eminence to the right of the road, crowned by horsemen. On our moving towards them, they descended into the plain to the number of about fifty, apparently with the design of attacking us; but upon my forming my men, and advancing, they retired leisurely by the road leading to Khelat,—halting occasionally and forming up also, as if to attack us, but again retiring on our approach, after firing a few shots without any effect. This system was continued until we had entered a small pass leading through the hills by which Khelat is surrounded, when the enemy once more formed, and suffered us to advance within fifty yards of them, as if here determined to oppose our further progress. They then fired a volley, wheeled, and gallopped off, fortunately for us, without waiting to see the result of their bravado, which had sent every man of our escort, saving the Jemadar, to the right about! Had our opponents followed up their advantage, Lieutenant Ramsey and myself would have been left to stand our ground as we best might, but it so turned out that the enemy continued their flight to Khelat, upon perceiving which our party recovered courage, and followed them a short distance. Our march this day was fifteen miles over a good road. During the night the troops were kept on the alert in anticipation either of an attack on the part of the garrison, or of a *chuppao* from the Noshky reinforcements expected from our rear.

13th. Marched at sunrise, the Local Horse being left in charge of the baggage. About a mile from the encampment we had just left, we were met by a body of about one hundred horse, who kept aloof, until they observed that we had no Cavalry to oppose to them, whereupon they became bolder, and, gallopping close up to the head of the column, discharged their matchlocks. A party of Light Infantry having been thrown out to keep them at distance, we continued our march, without further molestation, about six miles, when, on our surmounting a small range of hills, the town and fortress of Khelat suddenly burst upon our view. It was truly an imposing sight. Some small hills in front were crowned with masses of soldiers, and the towering citadel, which frowned above them in their rear, was completely clustered over with human beings,— ladies of the harem chiefly, who had assembled to witness the discomfiture of the Feringees, and the prowess of their Lords, all of whom, with the Khan at their head, had previously marched out to the heights, where they awaited us in battle array!

No sooner had the head of the British Column showed itself, than the enemy's guns, of which there were five in position on the heights, opened upon it; but, being ill-directed, they were unattended with effect. In order to assemble every efficient man of his small army, General Willshire here halted the troops, until the baggage had closed up, assigning the charge of it, and of the sick, to the Local Horse. It was very evident that the enemy, who greatly outstripped us in point of numbers, were fully bent upon mischief; and our total strength, amounting to less than one thousand bayonets, we had nothing to spare in the contest that awaited us. During this delay two companies were sent to clear some gardens on our left; and a body of horse threatening us from that direction, a few shrapnel shells were thrown amongst them, which caused them to withdraw to the fort. The cool and determined demeanour of our veteran General inspired every one present with confidence of success, nor shall I ever forget the obvious feeling of delight with which his deep-toned word of command, 'Loosen cartridges,' was received by the soldiers—evincing, as it did, that an immediate attack was intended, and that serious opposition might be expected.

The following plan of assault was then communicated by the General. Under cover of the Artillery, the three redoubts on the heights are first to be carried by four companies of each Regiment. Two companies are to advance through the gardens, on our left, the remaining ten companies are to form the reserve. The heights once in our possession would serve in a great measure to cover our camp from the Artillery of the fort, and would afford us a commanding position from which to annoy the Garrison.

CHAPTER XXI.

CAPTURE OF KHELAT.

All being in readiness, the three columns of attack moved steadily forward, preceded by the Artillery, which unlimbered at the foot of the hills, and opened a cannonade of shells and shrapnel with such admirable precision, that the masses of the enemy, crowning the heights, were compelled to abandon their position long before the Infantry had gained the summit. Observing the enemy endeavouring to draw off their guns, the General despatched me with orders to the Column of the Queen's Royals, which was the nearest to the gate, to pursue the fugitives, and, if possible, to enter the fort with them—but at any rate to prevent their taking in the ordnance. I overtook the head of the column before it had attained to the redoubt (C.) and gallopped on to the redoubt (D.) at the very moment that the enemy were vacating it; when, perceiving them to be engaged in an attempt to carry off one of the pieces of Artillery, I called on Captain Raitt, of the Queen's Royals, to push down quickly with his Grenadiers, and if unable to enter the gate with the enemy, at all events to capture the gun. I accompanied this party, which rushed down the hill, but arrived too late to enter the Fort with the enemy, who, however, abandoned the gun outside, and hastily closed the gate after them.

Leaving the Grenadiers to take post under cover of a ruined building, (marked E. in the plan,) within sixty yards of the gate, so as to be in readiness to enter by it, in case the General might decide upon following up this advantage by blowing open the gate before the Garrison should find time to block it up, as they doubtless would do, were the attack to be delayed, I rode back, to report progress. The whole of our troops were already on the heights, and the guns were also being dragged up. Four of the latter were directed to play upon the towers commanding the gateway from the positions B. B., whilst the other two were ordered down to D. for the purpose of battering the gate itself. The General at the same time despatched me to G., with instructions to bring up the Light Companies under Major Pennycuick to H.,* where a mud wall, about four feet in height, afforded shelter within thirty yards of the wall, on the opposite side of the gate to that near which the Grenadiers of the Queen's Royals were posted. Having brought them at double quick time across the plain to within two hundred yards of the walls, and then directed them to scatter and rush under cover, I returned to the General, taking the

* In order to avoid prolixity, this operation is alluded to in General Willshire's despatch, as though it had been simultaneous with the occupation of the position E.—I, however, took up both parties separately in the manner here described.

point E. in my way, in order to warn the Grenadiers that the gate would be immediately blown open, when they were to rush in simultaneously with the Light Companies from the opposite side. It was whilst taking up the positions E. and H. that most of the casualties during this day occurred, the troops so engaged being exposed to an exceedingly hot fire from the walls. On these two occasions I was the only mounted officer present; but although both the nature of my occupation, and the singularity of my rifle uniform, differing as it did from all others, must have attracted a considerable share of the enemy's observation, I escaped with my usual good fortune.

From the point D., the two guns now opened upon the gate, and being admirably directed (by Lieut. Henry Creed of the Bombay Artillery,) a few rounds were sufficient to throw down one half of it. The General's signals for the advance of the storming parties, not being immediately observed, I gallopped down, and accompanied the Grenadiers to the gate; after seeing them in secure occupation of which, I returned to the General, whom I met close to the fort, bringing up the main body of the troops. He immediately despatched me with Captain Darley's Company of H. M's. 17th Foot, with instructions to take the 31st Regiment Bengal Native Infantry along with me, and with these to storm the heights and secure the gate on the opposite side of the fort. After passing quickly round the western face, from which we were exposed to a considerable fire, I placed the Company of the 17th under cover of a spur of the hill, and thence proceeded back to seek for the 31st Regiment, which I found scouring the suburbs. Having united the two detachments, we stormed the heights at K, where we experienced some trifling opposition from matchlock=men occupying the rocks above: these being soon dispersed, we rushed down to the gate L. driving in a party of the enemy with such precipitation that they had not time to secure the gate, possession of which was thus obtained, and the escape of the Garrison entirely cut off.

We were here joined by a party under Major Deshon, which had been sent round by the eastern face of the fort. When I directed the officers to leave a detachment in charge of the gate, and with the remaining portion to make their way up to the citadel, which still maintained a fire upon our troops, whilst I accompanied Lieutenant Creed for the purpose of selecting a position from whence to bombard it with the Shah's guns. Placed the guns in position at N, and opened a fire on the citadel, which was continued with destructive effect, until our soldiers had obtained possession. Rejoining the General in the meantime, to report progress, I found him at the gate first carried, giving orders for attaching bags of gunpowder to the gates of the citadel, which had hitherto successfully resisted all attempts to enter it from this side. Reported that the party from the opposite quarter had already got well up, and with the aid of Lieutenant Creed's guns, would shortly surmount every obstacle. Hereupon troops were again sent up to co-operate, and a few minutes more sufficed to display the British standards waving over the highest of the towers of Khelat. All hostilities immediately ceased, and the soldiers displayed much greater forbearance than they usually do on such occasions. Quarter was never refused by them when craved by cries of 'Aman' 'Aman,' and before nightfall nearly two thousand prisoners had been removed from the fort unharmed.

About four hundred of the Garrison are supposed to have fallen in this affair, and amongst them are the chiefs Mehrab Khan, Wullee Mahommed Khan, and other principal Beloche chieftains—every person of note having been either slain or captured. Some anxiety was expressed by the General on the occasion of my rejoining him at the first gate, in consequence of the rumoured escape of Mehrab Khan; but I assured him that, as the fighting portion of the Garrison had been driven back whilst in the act of attempting to decamp by the opposite gate, I entertained no doubt that the Khan was still within the fort, since he could not, in honour, have previously deserted his followers. This afterwards proved to be the case. Foiled on that occasion, in his attempt to escape, the Chief had returned to the citadel with Wullee Mahommed Khan of Wudd, and others of his most trusty followers, where they had all died sword in hand; the Khan himself being slain by a shot through the neck, from whose hand it is not known. Considering the small number of our troops, not one half of whom were actually engaged, the loss on our side is severe. Thirty-two were killed, and one hundred and seven wounded; amongst the former is Lieutenant Gravatt of the Queen's Royals, and there are nine officers amongst the latter.

14th. Working parties have been employed the whole day in removing and burying the dead, as well in collecting prize property. Scattered as the dead bodies are over every part of the town, among houses, the numerous dark chambers of which are not easily explored, it has not yet been practicable to ascertain the number of the slain. The amount of booty is supposed to be very considerable; but we unfortunately do not possess the means of carrying it away, nor is there any market here, in which to dispose of it. The arms especially are of very superior manufacture, and the sword of the fallen chief Mehrab Khan in particular, which is of the most costly workmanship, is estimated to be of great value. The members of our little army have with one accord resolved upon presenting this enviable trophy to their gallant leader, General Willshire, in token of their admiration of his heroic bearing yesterday.*

* Vide Appendix.

CHAPTER XXII.

JOURNEY FROM KHELAT TO SONMEANEE.

14th ~~October~~ *November*. Having been relieved from military duty by the successful termination of hostilities, consequent on the capture of Khelat, and honored also by being made the bearer of General Willshire's despatches for the Bombay Government, I have resolved on making my way in disguise by the most direct route to Sonmeanee, the sea-port of Lus, and thence to embark for Curachee *en route* to Bombay. It is a point of great importance to ascertain the existence or otherwise of a practicable road for troops from Candahar and Shawl, through Belochistan, viâ Khelat to the sea; and that by Wudd having already been reported upon by Colonel Pottinger thirty years since, I have determined on exploring the road through Nal, which is said to be the better Kafila route of the two.

15th. My preparations being scarcely completed, I had intended to delay until to-morrow, but in the forenoon two holy Syuds of Shawl, who had consented to accompany me, came to urge my departure, in order, they said, that we might precede, if possible, the tidings of the death of the Chiefs Wullee Mahommed Khan of Wudd, and Shah Dost Khan of Nal, both of whom had been slain in the combat of the 13th, and it being moreover considered advisable to depart as secretly as possible, we agreed to leave camp at midnight. Having accordingly disguised myself in Affghan costume, and being accompanied by the two Syuds aforesaid, together with two armed attendants of theirs, and one servant of my own, we left the British camp in the dead of night, the whole party of six persons being mounted on four ponies and two camels, carrying provisions for ourselves, and as much grain for the animals as we could conveniently take.

16th. Nineteen hours in the saddle. Halted at 4 A. M. for an hour at Rodinje, after a pleasant, though bitterly cold march of four hours under moonlight. It being usual for the inhabitants of this district to migrate during the winter to the warmer climate of Cutch Gundava, we found not a soul in the village. At day-break resumed our journey to Sohrab, a cluster of villages also deserted for the same reason, except by one or two families, which had remained in each to look after the premises. During this day's march we passed many groups of fugitive women from Khelat, the men, who ought to have protected them, having either been slain in the conflict, or contrived to outstrip their wives in flight. One party however was better attended than the others, being accompanied by several armed men; but even here, with the exception of one old lady, all the females were on foot. By these my friends the

Syuds were recognised as old acquaintances, and a long detail was entered into by the ladies of the hardships they had endured. They proved to be the families of Mehrab Khan's brother, and of his principal minister, Mahommed Hoossain Khan, and none of them, poor things, had ever before been beyond the precincts of a harem. It behoved us while we kept the same road to remain with this party a sufficient time to listen to all their griefs, and having been previously introduced by my companions in the character of a Peer, which holy disguise I had afterwards to support during the whole journey, I was most especially called upon to sympathise in their woes. This I did by assuming an air of deep gravity and attention, although in reality I did not understand a single word that was uttered, and in the meanwhile one of my companions relieved the mother for a time of the burthen of Mahommed Hoossain Khan's infant child, which he carried before him on the saddle.

During the time that we accompanied this party, it may be imagined that my situation was far from being an enviable one. Independently of the fairness of my complexion, which, although concealed as much as possible by a large turban bound over the chin, was eminently calculated to excite suspicion, it so happened that I had equipped both myself and my servant with raiment taken from Mahommed Hoossain Khan's own wardrobe, from amongst the contents of which the prize agents had permitted me to select whatever was necessary for my disguise. Most fortunately indeed I had conceived the humblest garb to be the best suited to the pious character I was to sustain; and the apparel I had chosen was, therefore, in all probability, of too common a description to have passed through the harem, by the fair hands of the inmates of which, the more costly suits are wont to be embroidered. Whether from this circumstance, or because weightier cares diverted their thoughts from such trifles, our garments were not recognised, and we took the very first opportunity of pleading an excuse to leave the poor creatures in the rear. We were pestered nevertheless throughout the journey, by horsemen gallopping up from different directions to enquire the particulars of the Khelat disaster; but my friends the Syuds always contrived to place themselves in such a position as to be the first questioned; when they found so much of interest to communicate to the enquirers, that I remained altogether unnoticed.

The sensation created by the news of the overthrow of Khelat, and by the fate of Mehrab Khan with his chiefs and vassals, was very great; and so far as I could comprehend, many were the curses poured out upon the heads of the Feringees, and numerous were the vows of vengeance and retaliation to which the auditors gave utterance—their national vanity, the while, inducing them to employ every argument by which to excuse the complete defeat of their countrymen. The more they interrogated, however, the more were they downhearted at the undeniable evidence that had been given of Feringee prowess; and although we were informed that the Khan's brother, (who with his spiritual adviser

yesterday passed us in flight,) had publicly given
out that he was proceeding to assemble the tribes,
in order to assail our troops during their descent
through the passes, I am strongly inclined to the
belief, that their ardour to avenge the cause of their
Beloche brethren, has been so considerably cooled
by what they have learned, that it will shortly eva-
porate altogether.

For our bivouac this night we selected the walls
of a deserted village, hoping under their friendly
shelter to escape observation; but our arrival was
perceived, and notwithstanding the apparently deserted state of the country, inquisitive persons
flocked round us to institute inquiries respecting relatives or friends who had been engaged at Khelat.
Amongst many others were certain agents, who had
been sent back by the brother of the deceased Khan,
to meet and escort his own family and that of the
minister, with whom we had *forgathered* in the
morning. The worthy Syuds, my companions, were
by no means sparing of their taunts at the conduct
of the Khan's brother, who had ignominiously fled
on horseback with his associates, leaving his family
to trudge behind on foot; nor did they omit to hint
that he must have been somewhat precipitate in his
retreat from Khelat, inasmuch as there was no
egress from that place for a full hour before Mehrab
Khan's fall in the citadel. This sally on the part of
my friends did not fail to elicit considerable mirth
in the assembly; and the emissaries of the Khan's
brother, whose name has escaped me, looked somewhat foolish thereat. They, however, talked very

largely, and asserted that the Khan had no other object in view than to raise the clans, and thus cut off the accursed Feringees in the pass. I subsequently enquired of the Syuds whether this was likely to be true, as in that case I should wish to send back in order to warn the General of the contemplated hostilities. They, however, assured me, that the blow which had been struck on the 13th would preclude all chance of any further obstruction being attempted to the British arms; and that whilst no body of Beloches would now venture to unite for the purpose of molesting the army, the Khan's brother had merely urged that pretext with a view of covering his own cowardice.

During the discussions which took place, I had, by pretending to be asleep, avoided the inconvenience of being personally questioned; but my companions were compelled to satisfy a whole string of interrogatories which lasted until the night was far advanced. The moment we were relieved from the irksome presence of company, therefore, instead of resting, as we had intended, until dawn, we resolved upon pushing on forthwith, with the design of avoiding the further detention which might be expected to accrue from the inconvenient cross-examination of a fresh set of visiters in the morning. An indigent native was here prevailed on to engage himself with us in capacity of guide; but only upon condition, that I would furnish him with a charm to preserve his sick camel from dying during his absence! A tuft of the animal's hair having accordingly been brought to me, I was obliged, in support of my assumed character, to go through the mummery of muttering over it a string of cabalistic words—may God forgive the hypocrisy!

We travelled other six hours during the night to a stream of clear water at which we bivouacked until the day broke. Resuming our journey in the morning, we were not a little rejoiced to find by the traces of horses and camels that the Khan's brother, and other fugitives whose route we had hitherto followed, and whose presence in our front had been the source of considerable anxiety, had now struck off to the left, and fallen into the high road to Wudd.

CHAPTER XXIII.

JOURNEY FROM KHELAT TO SONMEANEE,—CONTINUED.

On the 17th we continued our journey ten hours to Parkur, a village lately destroyed by the Khan of Khelat, for some contumacy on the part of its inhabitants. Here, among the ruins, we found a comfortable asylum for the night, and were exempted from the society of strangers, of whom we fortunately met none during this day's march; the few hamlets that we had passed, being at this season entirely deserted.

18th. Seventeen hours on the road. Departing at daybreak, we crossed a high range of hills by a goat path impracticable for laden cattle. My companions having discovered that certain persons, whom they thought it prudent to avoid, were on the high road to Nal, we occupied five hours in reaching that place; and, having passed it, rested in the jungle, three miles beyond, sending one of the Syuds with the two armed attendants into the village to procure grain for our horses. This party unfortunately missing our place of concealment, subsequently passed on, and we waited for them in vain until the evening. The other Syud then became so uneasy, that he went back to the village to enquire for them, leaving me alone with my domestic Hoossain, to abide his return. As neither of us could speak a single syllable of the language of Belochistan, we should have been somewhat awkwardly situated, had we been discovered and addressed by any of the numerous inhabitants, who passed close to our hiding place on their way home from the fields. Fortunately, however, no one did perceive us. Nearly another hour having elapsed, and darkness coming on, without any appearance of the Syuds' return, I could not but conclude that my presence had been discovered, and that Fakeer Mahommed, the chief of Nal, whose near relation had been killed at the storm of Khelat, had adopted the plan of detaining my companions, in order to compel me to come to his village in search of them.

Under these circumstances, I considered what was best to be done. The whole of our money and provisions was with the absentees; and, destitute of these essentials—without a guide, and without the smallest knowledge of the language—our murder was inevitable at the hands of the very first Beloches we should meet, who could not fail immediately to penetrate our disguise. I determined, therefore, at once to proceed to the village, where, should I fail to terrify the chief into civility, by threats of the consequences of maltreating a British officer, I hoped that the holy influence of my Syud freinds might prove of some avail. We were on our way accordingly, and I was consoling poor Hoossain with the assurance that *his* life, as a Mahommedan, was at all events secure, when a cry from behind attracted our attention, and, looking round, we joyfully recognized our friend, the second Syud, who, having also missed our place of concealment, had long been hunting for us. His return brought a most welcome reprieve from what I considered almost certain destruction; and he informed us, that the rest of our party had left the village some hours previously, and had doubtless gone on, under the impression that we had preceded them. We therefore set out forthwith in search; and, after tracing them for two hours from village to village, at each of which we ascertained that they had also been seeking for us, we at length discovered them in a small fort assisting at the *coronach* for the dead Chief, the tidings of whose fall at Khelat had been received that very afternoon. Long before we reached this village, the wailing of the women had burst upon our ears at intervals, and amid the deep stillness of the night it had sounded very plaintively. The relatives of the deceased urgently pressed us to enter the house of mourning; but in the hour of such affliction we would not be prevailed on to obtrude ourselves, and, after resting an hour, were but too glad to take advantage of so good an excuse for resuming our journey.

Resolved to outstrip the news of the Khelat catastrophe, we now pushed on throughout the night at an ambling pace of at least five miles an hour—not once drawing bridle until the grey of the morning; having then travelled eight hours over a smooth and level road, which was lighted by a splendid moon. The weather has now become quite mild, and whilst it forms a most agreeable contrast to the bitter and pinching cold we have lately endured, serves to prove how greatly we must have descended since leaving Khelat. It is satisfactory also to find, that we have at least emerged from an inhabited country. Not a trace of any human habitation have we seen within the last thirty miles, and it is therefore with a feeling of much greater security than I hitherto permitted myself to indulge, that we are about to lie down on the banks of a river to obtain two hours' sleep.

19th. On awakening about 7 A. M. we were not a little vexed to find that our hired guide had decamped. He had unfortunately been paid in advance for the whole trip to Beila, as far as which town, he had engaged to escort us; and although invariably accommodated, like ourselves, with a seat on the back of a camel, he had probably become weary of the long journey, and had consequently taken advantage of our sound sleep to leave us in the lurch. As we were in the constant habit of sleeping above the little property that we possessed, and invariably held our horses' bridles in our hands, the fellow had happily departed without robbing us; and some flocks being observed at a little distance, we found means to persuade a shepherd to take his place, and accompany us in character of guide.

Our journey this day, which occupied eight hours, was by a good road, passing by easy ascents and declivities over a lofty range of mountains, styled the 'Oornach.' We bivouacked in the bed of the Oornach river, which is, generally speaking, dry; but a few small springs here trickled into it from the side of the hill, and forming a rill, the moisture around which had induced the growth of a little green grass. This was the first forage that we had possessed either the time or the opportunity to afford to our horses, the poor beasts having hitherto subsisted upon a scanty allowance of grain, brought with us from Khelat in the first instance, and afterwards replenished at Nal. Here also the camels found a little green tamarisk upon which to browse—a luxury which, for the first time during our journey, they had yesterday enjoyed in the valley of Nal. On our entering that valley the sight of the luxuriant green tamarisk bushes was really quite refreshing, forming as they did the most agreeable contrast to the brown and stunted vegetation of Affghanistan, which ever seems as though it had been scorched by fire or blighted by frost. With exception of a few juniper bushes in the Kakur hills, this was indeed the very first *green* foliage that I had seen since leaving Cabul; and its appearance, together with that of mat-rushes, and many familiar Indian trees, such as the Babool and the Neem, of which I had totally lost sight after entering Affghanistan, served not a little to enliven my last night's moonlight march. To me, even the scanty yellow grass, on the side of the hills which bound the Sohrab valley proved a gratifying sight; for nowhere betwixt that place and Cabul is grass to be found growing wild, saving where it occasionally fringes the running watercourses. During this day's march, we saw neither a human habitation nor a human being.

CHAPTER XXIV.

ARRIVAL AT SONMEANEE.

The moon was almost at the full, and we marched at midnight of the 20th.—In a sequestered dell lying in the very heart of the hills, and seemingly quite isolated from the rest of the world by the wild sterile mountains surrounding it, we passed several fields of juwarree—the first I had beheld since leaving India—and also some straggling hamlets. Notwithstanding the peaceful appearance of their secluded abode, the inhabitants of this valley are represented to be a particularly wild and savage race, and we therefore passed silently on our way, without communicating with, or arousing a soul. We next surmounted the Poorallee range, which appears to be higher than that styled Oornach: and here my hopes of the practicability of this route, which had hitherto been sanguine, were completely extinguished. The road over this pass, which I saw no means of otherwise turning, is a path so narrow, steep, and rocky—sometimes winding along the sides of precipitous hills—at others through narrow fissures in hard rock—as to be utterly impracticable for guns, and incapable of being made so, unless at immense cost of time and labour, if at all.

We dismounted after having been eleven hours in the saddle, and passed the day in a ravine, which afforded a scanty supply of water, and a little green pasture for the cattle. Making a pretext of the heat, I here separated from my companions, and sought the shelter of a bush at a little distance, my real object being to indulge in the perusal of a Bombay Times newspaper of the 12th October, which I had secreted about my person for the purpose of beguiling a weary hour, but which I had hitherto found no opportunity of reading. The history of this paper is somewhat extraordinary. After the storm of Khelat, while the place was yet uncleared of the prisoners, and while some of the garrison were even still holding out, a person of consideration among the Beloches held it up to a party of our soldiers, who, deeming the act to be a barefaced avowal of the personal share he had taken in the plunder of some of our *dâks*, (the most vexatious of the many depredations that had been committed,) would, in all human probability, have immolated the supposed delinquent on the spot, had not an officer (Major Neil Campbell) fortunately passed at the very moment. By that gentleman it was ascertained that the holder of the newspaper had previously sent to tender his submission to the Political Agent, and to request of him a safe passport, when no writing materials being obtainable, a copy of the Times, that morning received, was, in lieu of a written document, placed in his hands to serve as an instrument of protection.

I was busily occupied with my paper when a rustling noise above me drew my attention; and looking up, I was not a little startled to find myself confronted by a ferocious-looking Beloche, who, armed with a long matchlock, was scanning me from the top of the bank. On my calling to my companions, who were seated at no great distance, and whom he saw rise immediately, the ruffian made off. How he came into that spot, or what his intentions were, I have not the slightest idea, but this rencontre served as a warning to me not to separate again from my companions, and to be more circumspect in future how I exhibited the newspaper.

In the evening, we continued our journey for seven hours over another mountain range, both the ascent and descent of which were easy. The road generally wound along smooth, firm, sandy beds of dry water channels, which, in their descent, gradually widened to the expanse of a magnificent river, though totally destitute of water. The banks are sometimes flanked by sloping hills, and skirted with shady tamarisk trees of gigantic growth—at others hemmed in by bare perpendicular rocks of great altitude. In the former case the hills generally open into wide valleys;—in the latter the iron girt walls contract to a narrow channel. Except in the secluded dell noticed above, not a trace of any inhabitant presented itself during this day's march, which lasted eighteen hours. The bold mountain scenery throughout the whole distance, alternately cast in deep shadow, and next lighted up by the brightest moonbeams, was striking and beautiful; and in many clumps of the "prickly pear" I had the pleasure of recognizing an old and familiar Indian acquaintance, which conjured up pleasing reminiscences of boar and tiger hunts, to "while the weary way."

21st. At break of day we arose from our bivouack, and continued to wind along the beds of dry water channels, from which, after two hours travelling, the road at last emerged, and right glad was I then to find my view to the southward unconfined by hills. All before me is now open; all difficulties are surmounted: and having outstripped the tidings of the fall of Khelat, there is little danger to be apprehended during the residue of the journey. An easy march of nine hours and a half has brought us to a hamlet on the opposite bank of the Poorallee, where we have bivouacked. It is a fine river, skirted by cultivation along the right bank for the last six miles of our route. My companions are here indulging in a fatted lamb, and having here cast off much of their former reserve, maintain free intercourse with the inhabitants. The daughter of Mehrab Khan being espoused by the Beila Chief, who is moreover the nephew of Wullee Mahommed Khan, it is of course an object, that the tragedy enacted at Khelat should still be kept a profound secret. In spite of all the feasting around me, my own fare continues to consist as heretofore of dates and water—it being requisite to keep up appearances, and not to infringe the abstinence befitting my holy character.

22d. In order that we might pass Beila before the day dawned, we started this morning at 3 A. M.

A large kafila of merchants and others from Bombay being encamped outside, under the walls of the town, we were obliged to pass through the midst of them. The leaders having been aroused by the barking of their dogs, and observing from what direction we came, were most clamorous and importunate for information as to the state of affairs at Khelat: they had heard in Bombay that the British army was shortly to arrive there, and were not a little apprehensive that in case of warfare, they might suffer in passing through the country. The Syuds, however, were prudently uncommunicative, and stoutly asserted that our party had come from Nal only; at the time of leaving which place it was uncertain, they said, how the Feringees would settle with Mehrab Khan. The merchants evidently suspected that we knew more about the matter than we chose to divulge, and for a considerable time continued to ply and pester us with an infinity of questions, nor was it until the day broke, we contrived to escape from their irksome catechising. By the inhabitants of Beila my friends were particularly anxious to avoid recognition, as they would have insisted on detaining us from motives of hospitality, which might have led to the most unpleasant consequences. Pursuing our journey until 1 P. M., we rested on the bank of the Porallee, at a spot where no village existed. From Beila there are two roads to Sonmeanee, and I determined on adopting that by Lyaree, the other, although more direct, having already been explored by Colonel Pottinger.

23d. We marched yesterday evening at 8 o'clock,

and after travelling throughout the night, and passing the paltry little village of Lyaree, reached Sonmeanee at 10 in the forenoon, having been fourteen hours in the saddle. Owing to the want of population, the whole tract of country which extends from Beila to the coast, although perfectly level, and containing a rich soil which is well watered by the Poorallee, is in fact little better than a desert. In addition to Beila, Lyaree, and Sonmeanee, half a dozen hamlets, each consisting of a few miserable huts, were the only human habitations that I saw between the hills and the sea.

In the Appendix the reader will find a detailed account of my route from Khelat to Sonmeanee, when I made myself known to the Hindoo Agent of Nao Mull of Curachee, who treated my companions and myself with great hospitality, and provided me with a boat. In it I embarked in the evening for Curachee, taking with me Affghan Yaboo, which, although not more than thirteen hands in height, had carried myself and my saddle bags, weighing altogether upwards of sixteen stone, the whole distance from Khelat—being three hundred and fifty-five miles—in seven days and a half, during which time I had passed one hundred and eleven hours on his back.

From Curachee I proceeded to Bombay, and not many days after my arrival there, a party of Beloche horse dealers also landed, who had embarked at Sonmeanee very shortly after my departure from that seaport. They state that at midnight of the evening on which I sailed, the son of Wullee Mahommed Khan (the Chief of Wudd, who was slain at the storm of Khelat), arrived in great haste with a party in pursuit of me; and, on learning that I had already gone, displayed extreme disappointment and irritation. It would appear, that information of my journey and disguise had been received by this chief the day after I passed through Nal. To the forced march of fifty miles, therefore, which was made thence by our party, with the design of outstripping the flying tidings of the overthrow of Khelat, I may consider myself principally indebted for my escape— my pursuers having missed me at the seaport of Sonmeanee, only by a few hours.

CHAPTER XXV.

CONCLUSION.

LETTER FROM THE ENVOY AT CABUL.

When this volume had nearly passed through the press, I was honored with the following communication from the principal British authority in the countries which formed the scene of the late Campaign; and as it refers to some of the statements contained in the preceding pages, its introduction at this place, as a conclusion to my journal, will not probably be deemed inappropriate.

To Captain Outram,
&c. &c. &c.

'Sir,—I am desired by His Majesty Shah Shooja ool Moolk, to convey to you his acknowledgment of the zeal, gallantry, and judgment displayed by you in several instances during the past year, whilst employed in his Majesty's immediate service.

'His Majesty desires me to specify three instances, on which your merits and exertions were particularly conspicuous.

'First, on the occasion of your gallantry in placing yourself at the head of his Majesty's troops engaged in dispersing a large body of rebels who had taken up a threatening position immediately above His Majesty's encampment on the day previous to the storm of Ghizni.

'Secondly, on the occasion of your commanding the party sent in pursuit of Dost Mahommed Khan, when your zealous exertions would in all probability have been crowned with success, but for the treachery of your Affghan associates.

'And thirdly, for the series of able and successful operations, conducted under your superintendence, which ended in the subjection or dispersion of certain rebel Ghiljee and other tribes, and which have had the effect of tranquillizing the whole line of country between Cabul and Candahar, where plunder and anarchy had before prevailed.

'For these signal and important services His Majesty has commanded me to signify to you that he has been pleased to confer upon you the Second Class of the order of the Douranee Empire, as a mark of his royal approbation.

'I have the honor to be, &c.'

(Signed) W. H. MACNAGHTEN,

Envoy and Minister.

Jellabad, 7th January, 1840.

APPENDIX.

APPENDIX.

No. 1.

DECLARATION

OF THE RIGHT HONOURABLE THE GOVERNOR-GENERAL OF
INDIA, ON THE ASSEMBLY OF THE ARMY OF THE INDUS.

Simla, October 1, 1838.

The Right Honourable the Governor-General of India having, with the concurrence of the Supreme Council, directed the assemblage of a British Force, for service across the Indus, His Lordship deems it proper to publish the following exposition of the reasons which have led to this important measure.

It is a matter of notoriety, that the treaties entered into by the British Government, in the year 1832, with the Ameers of Sinde, the Nawab of Bahawulpore, and Maha Raja Runjeet Singh, had for their object, by opening the navigation of the Indus, to facilitate the extension of commerce, and to gain for the British nation, in Central Asia, that legitimate influence which an interchange of benefits would naturally produce.

With a view to invite the aid of the *de facto* Rulers of Affghanistan to the measures necessary for giving full effect to those treaties, Captain Burnes was deputed, towards the close of the year 1836, on a mission to Dost Mahommed Khan, the Chief of Cabool. The original objects of that officer's mission were purely of a commercial nature. Whilst Captain Burnes, however, was on his journey to Cabool, information was received by the Governor-General, that the troops of Dost Mahommed Khan had made a sudden and unprovoked attack on those of our ancient ally, Maha Raja Runjeet Singh. It was naturally to be apprehended that His Highness the Maha Raja would not be slow to avenge this aggression; and it was to be feared that the flames of war, being once kindled in the very regions into which we were endeavouring to extend our commerce, the peaceful and beneficial purposes of the British Government would be altogether frustrated. In order to avert a result so calamitous, the Governor-General resolved, on authorizing Captain Burnes, to intimate to Dost Mahommed Khan that, if he should evince a disposition to come to just and reasonable terms with the Maha Raja, His Lordship would exert his good offices with His Highness for the restoration of an amicable understanding between the two powers. The Maha Raja, with the characteristic confidence which he has uniformly placed in the faith and friendship of the British nation, at once assented to the proposition of the Governor-General, to the effect that, in the meantime, hostilities on his part should be suspended.

It subsequently came to the knowledge of the Governor-General, that a Persian Army was besieging Herat; that intrigues were actively prosecuted throughout Affghanistan, for the purpose of extending Persian influence and authority to the banks of, and even beyond, the Indus; and that the Court of Persia had not only commenced a course of injury and insult to the Officers of Her Majesty's Mission in the Persian territory, but had afforded evidence of being engaged in designs wholly at variance with the principles and objects of its alliance with Great Britain.

After much time spent by Captain Burnes in fruitless negotiation at Cabool, it appeared that Dost Mahommed Khan, chiefly in consequence of his reliance upon Persian encouragement and assistance, persisted, as respected his misunderstanding with the Sikhs, in urging the most unreasonable pretensions, such as the Governor-General could not, consistently with justice, and his regard for the friendship of Maha Raja Runjeet Singh, be the channel of submitting to the consideration of His Highness; that he avowed schemes of aggrandisement and ambition, injurious to the security and peace of the frontiers of India; and that he openly threatened, in furtherance of those schemes, to call in every foreign aid which he could command. Ultimately he gave his undisguised support to the Persian designs of Affghanistan, of the unfriendly and injurious character of which, as concerned the British Power in India, he was well apprized, and by his utter disregard of the views and interests of the British Government, compelled Captain Burnes to leave Cabool without having effected any of the objects of his Mission.

It was now evident, that no further interference could be exercised by the British Government to bring about a good understanding between the Sikh Ruler and Dost Mahommed Khan, and the hostile policy of the latter Chief showed too plainly that, so long as Cabool remained under his government, we could never hope that the tranquillity of our neighbourhood would be secured, or that the interests of our Indian Empire would be preserved inviolate.

The Governor-General deems it in this place necessary to revert to the siege of Herat, and the conduct of the Persian nation. The siege of that city has now been carried on by the Persian Army for many months. The attack upon it was a most unjustifiable and cruel aggression, perpetrated and continued, notwithstanding the solemn and repeated remonstrances of the British Envoy at the Court of Persia, and after every just and becoming offer of accommodation had been made and rejected. The besieged have behaved with a gallantry and fortitude worthy of the justice of their cause, and the Governor-General would yet indulge the hope, that their heroism may enable them to maintain a successful defence until succours shall reach them from British India. In the meantime, the ulterior designs of Persia, affecting the interests of the British Government, have been, by a succession of events, more and more openly manifested. The Governor-General has recently ascertained by an official despatch from Mr. Mc.Neil, Her Majesty's Envoy, that His Excellency has been compelled, by the refusal of his just demands, and by a systematic course of disrespect adopted towards him by the Persian Government, to quit the Court of the Shah, and to make a public declaration of the cessation of all intercourse between the two Governments. The necessity under which Great Britain is placed, of regarding the present advance of the Persian Arms into Affghanistan as an act of hostility towards herself, has also been officially communicated to the Shah, under the express order of Her Majesty's Government.

The Chiefs of Candahar (brothers of Dost Mahommed Khan of Cabool), have vowed their adherence to the Persian Policy, with the same full knowledge of its opposition to the rights and interests of the British nation in India, and have been openly assisting in the operations against Herat.

In the crisis of affairs consequent upon the retirement of our Envoy from Cabool, the Governor-General felt the importance of taking immediate measures for arresting the rapid progress of foreign intrigue and aggression towards our own territories.

His attention was naturally drawn at this conjuncture to the position and claims of Shah Shooja ool Moolk, a Monarch who, when in power, had cordially acceded to the measures of united resistance to external enmity, which were at that time judged necessary by the British Government, and who, on his Empire being usurped by its present Ruler, had found an honourable asylum in the British Dominions.

It had been clearly ascertained, from the information furnished by the various officers who have visited Affghanistan, that the Barukzye Chiefs, from their disunion and unpopularity, were ill fitted, under any circumstances, to be useful Allies to the British Government, and to aid us in our just and necessary measures of national defence. Yet so long as they refrained from proceedings injurious to our interests and security, the British Government acknowledged and respected their authority. But a different policy appeared to be now more than justified by the conduct of those Chiefs, and to be indispensable to our own safety. The welfare of our possessions in the East requires that we should have on our Western Frontier, an Ally, who is interested in resisting aggression, and establishing tranquillity, in the place of Chiefs ranging themselves in subservience to a hostile power, and seeking to promote schemes of conquest and aggrandizement.

After serious and mature deliberation, the Governor-General was satisfied, that a pressing necessity, as well as every consideration of policy and justice, warranted us in espousing the cause of Shah Shooja ool Moolk, whose popularity throughout Affghanistan had been proved to his Lordship by the strong and unanimous testimony of the best authorities. Having arrived at this determination, the Governor-General was further of opinion, that it was just and proper, no less from the position of Maha Raja Runjeet Singh, than from his undeviating friendship towards the British Government, that His Highness should have the offer of becoming a party to the contemplated operations. Mr. Macnaghten was accordingly deputed, in June last, to the Court of His Highness, and the result of his mission has been the conclusion of a Tripartite Treaty, by the British Government, the Maha Raja, and Shah Shooja ool Moolk, whereby His Highness is guaranteed in his present possessions, and has bound himself to co-operate for the restoration of the Shah to the throne of his ancestors. The friends and enemies of any one of the contracting parties have been declared to be the friends and enemies of all. Various points have been adjusted, which had been the subjects of discussion between the British Government and His Highness the Maha Raja, the identity of whose interests with those of the Honorable Company has now been made apparent to all the surrounding States. A guaranteed independence will, upon favorable conditions, be tendered to the Ameers of Sinde; and the integrity of Herat, in the possession of its present Ruler, will be fully respected; while, by the measures completed, or in progress, it may reasonably be hoped, that the general freedom and security of commerce will be promoted; that the name and just influence of the British Government will gain their proper footing among the Nations of Central Asia; that tranquillity will be established upon the most important Frontier of India; and that a lasting barrier will be raised against hostile intrigue and encroachment.

His Majesty Shah Shooja ool Moolk will enter Affghanistan, surrounded by his own troops, and will be supported against foreign interference, and factious opposition, by a British Army. The Governor-General confidently hopes that the Shah will be speedily replaced on his Throne, by his own subjects and adherents, and, when once he shall be secured in power, and the independence and integrity of Affghanistan established, the British Army will be withdrawn. The Governor-General has been led to these measures, by the duty which is imposed upon him of providing for the security of the possessions of the British Crown, but he rejoices that, in the discharge of this duty, he will be enabled to assist in restoring the union and prosperity of the Affghan people. Throughout the approaching operations, British influence will be sedulously employed to further every measure of general benefit; to reconcile differences; to secure oblivion of injuries; and to put an end to the distractions by which, for so many years, the welfare and happiness of the Affghans have been impaired. Even to the Chiefs, whose hostile proceedings have given just cause of offence to the British Government, it will seek to secure liberal and honorable treatment, on their tendering early submission, and ceasing from opposition to that course of measures, which may be judged the most suitable for the general advantage of their country.

By order of the Right Honorable the Governor-General of India.

(Signed)   W. H. MACNAGHTEN,
Secy. to the Govt. of India, with the Gov.-Genl.

NOTIFICATION.

With reference to the preceding declaration, the following appointments are made.

Mr. W. H. Macnaghten, Secretary to Government, will assume the functions of Envoy and Minister, on the part of the Government of India at the Court of Shah Shooja ool Moolk. Mr. Macnaghten will be assisted by the following officers.

Captain Alexander Burnes, of the Bombay Establishment, who will be employed, under Mr. Macnaghten's directions, as Envoy to the Chiefs of Khelat, or other States.

Lieutenant E. D'Arcy Todd, of the Bengal Artillery, to be Political Assistant and Military Secretary to the Envoy and Minister.

Lieutenant Eldred Pottinger, of the Bombay Artillery; Lieutenant R. Leech, of the Bombay Engineers, Mr. P. B. Lord, of the Bombay Medical Establishment, to be Political Assistants to ditto ditto.

Lieutenant E. B. Conolly, of the 6th Regiment Bengal Cavalry, to command the escort of the Envoy and Minister, and to be Military Assistant to ditto ditto.

Mr. G. J. Berwick, of the Bengal Medical Establishment, to be Surgeon to ditto ditto.

(Signed)   W. H. MACNAGHTEN.

No. 2.

CANDAHAR.

GENERAL ORDERS BY HIS EXCELLENCY LIEUTENANT-GE-
NERAL SIR JOHN KEANE, K. C. B., G. C. H., COMMANDING
THE ARMY OF THE INDUS.

Head-Quarters, Camp Candahar, May 4, 1839.

1. The combined forces of Bengal and Bombay, being now assembled at Candahar, the Commander-in-Chief congratulates all ranks on the triumphant though arduous march which they have accomplished, from distant and distinct parts of India, with a regularity and discipline which is much appreciated by him, and reflects upon themselves the highest credit. The difficulties which have been surmounted have been of no ordinary nature, and the recollection of what has been overcome must, hereafter, be a pleasing reflection to those concerned, who have so zealously, and in so soldierlike a manner, contributed to effect them, so as to arrive at the desired end. The Engineers had to make roads, and, occasionally, in some extraordinary steep mountain-passes, over which no wheeled carriage had ever passed. This was a work requiring science, and much severe labour; but so well has it been done, that the progress of the Army was in no manner impeded. The heavy and light ordnance were alike taken over in safety, by the exertions and good spirit of the Artillery, in which they were most cheerfully and ably assisted by the troops, both European and Native, and in a manner which gave the whole proceeding the appearance that each man was working for a favourite object of his own.

2. His Excellency shares in the satisfaction which those

troops must feel (after the difficult task they have accomplished, and the trying circumstances under which they have been placed, the nature of which is well known to themselves, and, therefore, unnecessary for him to detail), at knowing the enthusiasm with which the population of Candahar have received and welcomed the return of their lawful sovereign, Shah Shooja ool Moolk, to the throne of his ancestors in Affghanistan. Sir John Keane will not fail to report to the Right Honourable Lord Auckland, Governor-General of India, his admiration of the conduct and discipline of the troops, by which means it has been easy to effect, and to fulfil, the plans of his Lordship, in the operations of the campaign hitherto.

3. The Commander-in-Chief has already, in a G. O., dated the 6th ultimo, expressed his acknowledgment to Major-General Sir Willoughby Cotton, for the creditable and judicious manner in which he conducted the Bengal column, to the valley of Shawl. His Excellency has now a pleasing duty to perform, in requesting Major-General Willshire, commanding the Bombay column, to accept his best thanks for his successful exertions in bringing the troops of that Presidency to this ground, in the most efficient and soldier-like state.

4. The Commander-in-Chief entertains a confident expectation that the same orderly conduct, which has gained for the troops the good-will of the inhabitants of the states and countries through which they have passed, will continue to be observed by them during their advance upon Cabool, when the proper time for the adoption of that step shall have been decided upon by His Excellency, in concert with His Majesty Shah Shooja ool Moolk, and the Envoy and Minister, W. H. Macnaghten, Esq., representing British interests at the Court of the King of Affghanistan.

May 5.

On the occasion of His Majesty Shah Shooja ool Moolk

taking possession of his Throne, and receiving the homage of his people of Candahar, the following ceremonial will be observed :—

The whole of the troops, now at head-quarters, will be formed, in order of review, at daylight, on the morning of the 8th instant, on ground which will be pointed out to Assistants-Adjutants-General of Divisions, to-morrow afternoon, at five o'clock, by the Deputy-Adjutant-General of the Bengal Army.

The troops will take up their ground in the following order from the right.

Bengal.—Horse Artillery, Cavalry Brigade, Camel Battery, 1st Brigade of Infantry, 4th Brigade of Infantry.

Bombay.—Horse Artillery, Cavalry Brigade, Infantry Brigade.

The 4th Local Horse will take up a position in front of the right flank, and the Poona Auxiliary Horse in front of the left flank, for the purpose of keeping the space in advance of the troops clear of the populace.

A platform will be erected for His Majesty Shah Shooja ool Moolk, in front of the centre of the line, on either flank of which detachments of His Majesty's Cavalry will take post, to prevent the intrusion of the populace.

Captain Lloyd's Battery of Bombay Artillery will be stationed at the Edgah gate of the town, and will fire a royal salute as His Majesty passes.

The troops of His Majesty Shah Shooja will be drawn up in street, in the most convenient situation, between the gate and the British Army, and will salute His Majesty as he passes. The King's Artillery will be formed near the palace, and will fire a royal salute on the departure and return of His Majesty.

On His Majesty approaching the platform, a royal salute is to be fired from one of the batteries in the line; and, on his appearing in front of the troops, he will be received with a general salute from the whole line, the colours being lowered in the manner that is usual to crowned heads; and, as soon as the Infantry have shouldered arms, 101 guns are to be fired from the batteries in line, under directions from Brigadier Stevenson.

The Envoy and Minister, and officers attached to the mission, the Commander-in-Chief and his personal staff, and the officers at the heads of departments, and Affghan Sirdars, are to be stationed on the right of the throne, Syuds and Moollahs on the left, the populace on both sides and rear of the Shah, restrained by His Majesty's Cavalry, 4th Local Horse, and Poona Auxiliary Horse.

The Envoy and the Commander-in-Chief will present nuzzurs, as representatives of Government.

The officers of the Shah's Force will also present nuzzurs, leaving their troops for that purpose, after the Shah has passed, and returning to receive His Majesty.

The Shah's subjects will then present nuzzurs. At the close of the ceremony, the troops will march past, the Cavalry in columns of squadrons, the Infantry in columns of companies, in slow time; the columns will move up to the wheeling point in quick time. The columns, having passed, will continue their route towards the encampment, the 4th Brigade of Bengal Infantry moving on to the Cabool gateway, at which His Majesty will enter the city, where it will form a street, and salute His Majesty as he passes.

The troops are to appear in white trousers, the officers of the general staff in blue trousers and gold lace.

Corps will parade on the occasion as strong as possible, and the encampments will be protected by the convalescents, and by quarter and rear guards; such extra guards as may be considered essentially necessary, to be placed over treasure, at the discretion of Brigadiers, commanding Brigades.

Officers commanding divisions are to be supplied with field states, showing the actual number of troops there are under arms in their respective commands, to be delivered when called for.

His Majesty having expressed a wish that His Excellency the Commander-in-Chief should be near his person during the ceremony, Major-General Sir Willoughby Cotton will command the troops in line.

May 8.

Lieutenant-General Sir John Keane has received the gracious commands of His Majesty Shah Shooja ool Moolk to convey to Major-General Willshire, commanding in the field, to the Generals and other officers, and the non-commissioned officers and soldiers, who were present and assisted at the splendid spectacle of the King taking possession of his throne, this day, the deep sense His Majesty entertains of the obligations he owes to them and to the British nation. The King added, that he would request W. H. Macnaghten, Esq., Envoy and Minister at His Majesty's Court, to convey these his sentiments to the Right Honourable Lord Auckland, Governor-General of India.

No. 3.

GHIZNI.

GENERAL ORDERS BY THE RIGHT HONOURABLE THE GOVERNOR-GENERAL OF INDIA.

Secret Department.

Simla, 18th August, 1839.

The Right Honourable the Governor-General of India has great gratification in publishing for general information, a copy of a Report this day received from His Excellency Lieutenant-General Sir John Keane, K. C. B., Commander-in-Chief of the Army of the Indus, announcing the capture by storm, on the 23rd ultimo, of the important fortress of Ghuznee.

A salute of 21 guns will be fired on the receipt of this intelligence at all the principal stations of the Army in the three Presidencies.

By order of the Right Honourable the Governor-General of India.

T. H. MADDOCK,
Offg. Secy. to Govt. of India, with the G. G.

Head-Quarters, Camp Ghuznee, 24th July, 1839.
TO THE RIGHT HONOURABLE LORD AUCKLAND, G. C. B.
&c. &c. &c.

My Lord,—I have the satisfaction to acquaint your Lordship, that the Army under my command have succeeded in performing one of the most brilliant acts, it has ever been my lot to witness, during my service of 45 years in the four quarters of the globe, in the capture by storm of the strong and important fortress and citadel of Ghuznee yesterday.

It is not only that the Affghan nation, and I understand Asia generally, have looked upon it as impregnable, but it is in reality a place of great strength both by nature and art, far more so than I had reason to suppose, from any description that I received of it, although some are from officers in our own service, who had seen it in their travels.

I was surprised to find a high rampart in good repair, built on a scarped mound, about 35 feet high, flanked by numerous towers, and surrounded by a Fausse Braye and a wet ditch, whilst the height of the citadel covered the interior from the commanding fire of the hills from the north, rendering it nugatory. In addition to this screen, walls had been built before the gates, the ditch was filled with water and unfordable, and an outwork built on the right bank of the river, so as to command the bed of it.

It is therefore, the more honourable to the Troops, and must appear to the enemy out of all calculation extraordinary, that a fortress and citadel to the strength of which, for the last 30 years, they had been adding something each year, and which had a Garrison of 3,500 Affghan soldiers, commanded by Prince Mahommed Hyder, the son of Dost Mahommed Khan, the ruler of the country, with a commanding number of guns, and abundance of ammunition, and other stores, provisions, &c., for a regular siege, should have been taken by British science, and British valour, in less than two hours from the time the attack was made, and the whole, including the Governor and Garrison, should fall into our hands.

My despatch of the 20th instant, from Nanee, will have made known to your Lordship, that the camps of His Majesty Shah Shooja ool Moolk, and of Major-General Willshire with the Bombay troops, had there joined me, in accordance with my desire; and the following morning we made our march of twelve miles to Ghuznee, the line of march being over a fine plain, the troops were disposed in a manner that would have enabled me at any moment, had we been attacked, as was probable, from the large bodies of troops moving on each side of us, to have placed them in position to receive the enemy. They did not, however, appear; but, on our coming within range of the guns of the citadel and fortress of Ghuznee, a sharp cannonade was opened on our leading column, together with a heavy fire of musketry from behind garden walls, and temporary field works thrown up, as well as the strong outwork I have already alluded to, which commanded the bed of the river. From all but the outwork, the enemy were driven in, under the walls of the fort, in a spirited manner, by parties thrown forward by Major-General Sir W. Cotton, of the 16th and 48th Bengal Native Infantry, and Her Majesty's 13th Light Infantry, under Brigadier Sale. I ordered forward three troops of Horse Artillery, the Camel Battery, and one Foot Battery to open upon the citadel and fortress, by throwing shrapnell shells, which was done in a masterly style, under the direction of Brigadier Stevenson. My object in this, was to make the enemy show their strength in guns and other respects, which completely succeeded, and our shells must have done great execution, and occasioned great consternation. Being perfectly satisfied on the point of their strength in the course of half-an-hour, I ordered the fire to cease, and placed the troops in bivouac. A close reconnoissance of the place all round was then undertaken by Captain Thomson, the Chief Engineer, and Captain Peat, of the Bombay Engineers, accompanied by Major Garden, the Deputy-Quarter-Master-General of the Bengal Army, supported by a strong party of H. M.'s 16th Lancers, and one from H. M.'s 13th Light Infantry. On this party a steady fire was kept up, and some casualties occurred. Captain Thomson's report was very clear (he found the fortifications equally strong all round), and as my own opinion coincided with his, I did not hesitate a moment as to the manner in which our approach and attack upon the place should be made. Notwithstanding the march the troops had performed in the morning, and their having been a considerable time engaged with the enemy, I ordered the whole to move across the river (which runs close under the fort walls) in columns to the right and left of the town, and they were placed in position on the north side, on more commanding ground; and, securing the Cabool road, I had information that a night attack upon the camp was intended from without. Mahommed Ubzel Khan, the eldest son of Dost Mahommed Khan, had been sent by his father with a strong body of troops from Cabool, to the brother's assistance at Ghuznee, and was encamped outside the walls, but abandoned his position, on our approach, keeping, however, at the distance of a few miles from us. The two rebel Chiefs of the Ghiljee tribe, men of great influence, viz. Abdool Ruhman Khan, and Gool Mahommed Khan, had joined him with 1500 horse, and also a body of about 3000 Ghuznee, from Zeinat, under a mixture of Chiefs and Moolahs, carrying banners, and who had been assembled on the cry of a religious war: in short, we were in all directions surrounded by enemies. These last actually came down the hills on the 22d, and attacked the part of the camp occupied by His Majesty Shah Shooja and his troops, but were driven back with considerable loss, and banners taken.

At daylight, on the 22d, I reconnoitred Ghuznee, in company with the Chief Engineer, and the Brigadier commanding the Artillery, with the Adjutant and Quarter-Master-General of the Bengal Army, for the purpose of making all arrangements for carrying the place by storm, and these were completed in the course of the day. Instead of the tedious process of breaching (for which we were ill prepared), Captain Thomson undertook, with the assistance of Captain Peat, of the Bombay Engineers, Lieutenants Durand and Macleod, of the Bengal Engineers, and other officers under him (Captain Thomson), to blow in the Cabool gate (the weakest point) with gunpowder, and so much faith did I place on the success of this operation, that my plans for the assault were immediately laid down, and the orders given.

The different troops of Horse Artillery, the Camel and Foot Batteries, moved off their ground at 12 o'clock that night, without the slightest noise, as had been directed, and, in the most correct manner, took up the position assigned them, about 250 yards from the walls. In like manner, and with the same silence, the Infantry soon after moved from the ground, and all were at the post at the proper time. A few minutes before 3 o'clock in the morning, the explosion took place, and was completely successful. Captain Peat, of the Bombay Engineers, was thrown down and stunned by it, but shortly after recovered his senses and feeling. On hearing the advance sounded by the bugles (being the signal for the gate having been blown in), the Artillery, under the able direction of Brigadier Stevenson, consisting of Captain Grant's Troop of Bengal Horse Artillery, the Camel Battery, under Captain Abbot, both superintended by Major Pew, Captains Martin and Cotgrave's Troops of Bombay Horse Artillery, and Captain Lloyd's Battery of Bombay Foot Artillery, all opened a terrific fire upon the citadel and ramparts of the fort, and in a certain degree paralyzed the enemy.

Under the guidance of Captain Thomson, of the Bengal Engineers, the chief of the department, Colonel Dennie, of H. M.'s 13th Light Infantry, commanding the advance, consisting of the light companies of H. M.'s 2nd and 17th Foot, and of the Bengal European Regiment, with one company of H. M.'s 13th Light Infantry, proceeded to the gate, and, with great difficulty, from the rubbish thrown down, and the determined opposition offered by the enemy, effected an entrance, and established themselves within the gateway, closely followed by the main column, led, in a spirit of great gallantry, by Brigadier Sale, to whom I had entrusted the important post of commanding the storming party, consisting, (with the advance abovementioned) of H. M.'s 2d Foot, under Major Carruthers, the Bengal European Regiment, under Lieutenant-Colonel Orchard, followed by H. M.'s 13th Light Infantry, under Major Tronson, and H. M.'s 17th Regiment, under Lieutenant-Colonel Croker. The struggle within the fort was desperate for a considerable time. In addition to the heavy fire kept up, our troops were assailed by the enemy, sword in hand, and with daggers, pistols, &c., but British courage, perseverance, and fortitude, overcame all opposition, and the fire of the enemy in the lower area of the fort being nearly silenced, Brigadier Sale turned towards the citadel, from which could now be seen men abandoning the guns, running in all directions, throwing themselves down from immense heights, endeavouring to make their escape, and, on reaching the gate, with H. M.'s 17th, under Lieut.-Colonel Croker, followed by the 13th, forced it open,—at 5 o'clock in the morning, the colours of Her Majesty's 13th and 17th, were planted on the citadel of Ghuznee, amidst the cheers of all ranks. Instant protection was granted to the women found in the citadel (among whom were those of Mahommed Hyder, the Governor), and sentries placed over the Magazine for its security. Brigadier Sale reports having received much assistance from Captain Kershaw, of Her Majesty's 13th Light Infantry, throughout the whole of the service of the storming.

Major-General Sir W. Cotton executed, in a manner much to my satisfaction, the orders he had received. The Major-General followed closely the assaulting party into the fort, with the Reserve, namely, Brigadier Roberts, with the only available Regiment of his Brigade, the 35th Native Infantry, under Lieutenant-Colonel Monteath; part of Brigadier Sale's Brigade, the 16th Native Infantry, under Major MacLaren, and the 48th Native Infantry, under Lieutenant-Colonel Wheeler, and they immediately occupied the ramparts, putting down opposition whenever they met any, and making prisoners, until the place was completely in our possession. A desultory fire was kept up in the town, long after the citadel was in our hands, from those who had taken shelter in houses, and in desperation kept firing on all that approached them. In this way, several of our men were wounded, and some killed, but the aggressors paid dearly for their bad conduct, in not surrendering when the place was completely ours. I must not omit to mention that three companies of the 35th Native Infantry, under Captain Hay, ordered to the south side of the fort, to begin with a false attack to attract attention to that side, performed that service at the proper time, and greatly to my satisfaction.

As we were threatened with an attack for the relief of the Garrison, I ordered the 19th Bombay Native Infantry, under the command of Lieutenant-Colonel Stalker, to guard the Cabool road, and to be in support of the Cavalry Division. This might have proved an important position to occupy, but, as it was, no enemy appeared.

The Cavalry Division, under Major-General Thackwell, in addition to watching the approach of an enemy, had directions to surround Ghuznee, and to sweep the plain, preventing the escape of runaways from the Garrison. Brigadier Arnold's Brigade (the Brigadier himself, I deeply regret to say, was labouring under very severe illness, having shortly before burst a blood vessel internally, which rendered it wholly impossible for him to mount a horse that day), consisting of Her Majesty's 16th Lancers, under Lieutenant-Colonel Persse (momentarily commanding the Brigade, and Major Mac Dowell, the junior Major of the Regiment, the senior Major of the 16th Lancers, Major Cureton, an officer of great merit, being actively engaged in the execution of his duties as Assistant-Adjutant-General of the Cavalry Division), the 2d Cavalry, under Major Salter, and the 3rd, under Lieutenant-Colonel Smith, were ordered to watch the south and west sides. Brigadier Scott's Brigade was placed on the Cabool road, consisting of Her Majesty's 4th Light Dragoons, under Major Daly, and of the 1st Bombay Cavalry, under Lieutenant-Colonel Sandwith, to watch the north and east sides. This duty was performed in a manner greatly to my satisfaction.

After the storming, and that quiet was in some degree restored within, I conducted His Majesty Shah Shooja ool Moolk, and the British Envoy and Minister, Mr. Macnaghten, round the citadel, and a great part of the fortress. The King was perfectly astonished at our having made ourselves masters of a place, conceived to be impregnable when defended, in the short space of two hours, and in less than 48 hours after we came before it. His Majesty was of course greatly delighted at the result, when I afterwards, in the course of the day, took Mahommed Hyder Khan, the Governor, first to the British Minister, and then to the King, to make his submission. I informed His Majesty, that I made a promise that his life should not be touched, and the King, in very handsome terms, assented, and informed Mahommed Hyder, in my presence, that, although he and his family had been rebels, yet he was willing to forget and forgive all.

Prince Mahommed Hyder, the Governor of Ghuznee, is a prisoner of war in my camp, and under the surveillance of Sir Alexander Burnes—an arrangement very agreeable to the former.

From Major-General Sir Willoughby Cotton, commanding the 1st Native Infantry Division (of the Bengal Army), I have invariably received the strongest support, and, on this occasion, his exertions were manifest, in support of the honor of the profession and of our country.

I have likewise at all times received able assistance from Major-General Willshire, commanding the 2nd Infantry Division (of the Bombay Army), which it was found expedient on that day to break up, some for a storming party, and some for other duties; the Major-General, as directed, was in attendance upon myself.

To Brigadier Sale I feel deeply indebted, for the gallant and soldier-like manner in which he conducted the responsible and arduous duty entrusted to him, in command of the storming party, and for the arrangements he made in the citadel, immediately after taking possession of it. The sabre wound, which he received in the face, did not prevent his continuing to direct his column, until everything was secure, and I am happy in the opportunity of bringing to your Lordship's notice the excellent conduct of Brigadier Sale on this occasion.

Brigadier Stevenson, in command of the Artillery, was all I could wish, and he reports that Brigade-Majors Backhouse and Coghlan ably assisted him ; his arrangements were good, and the execution done by the Arm he commands, was such as cannot be forgotten by those of the enemy who have witnessed and survived it.

To Brigadier Roberts, to Colonel Dennie (who commanded the advance), and to the different officers commanding regiments already mentioned, as well as to the other officers and gallant soldiers under them, who so nobly maintained the honor and reputation of our country, my best acknowledgements are due.

To Captain Thomson, of the Bengal Engineers, the chief of the department with me, much of the credit of the success of this brilliant *coup-de-main* is due. A place of the same strength, and by such simple means as this highly-talented and scientific officer recommended to be tried, has perhaps never before been taken, and I feel I cannot do sufficient justice to Captain Thomson's merits for his conduct throughout. In the execution, he was ably supported by the officers already mentioned, and so eager were the other officers of the Engineers of both Presidencies for the honor of carrying the powder-bags, that the point could only be decided by seniority, which shews the fine feeling by which they are animated.

I must now inform your Lordship, that since I joined the Bengal Column in the valley of Shawl, I have continued my march with it in the advance, and it has been my good fortune to have had the assistance of two most efficient staff officers in Major Craigie, Deputy-Adjutant-General, and Major Garden, Deputy-Quarter-Master-General. It is but justice to those officers, that I should state to your Lordship, the high satisfaction I have derived from the manner in which all their duties have been performed up to this day, and that I look upon them as promising officers, to fill the higher ranks. To the other officers, of both departments, I am also much indebted, for the correct performance of all duties appertaining to their situations.

To Major Keith, the Deputy-Adjutant-General, and Major Campbell, the Deputy-Quarter-Master-General, of the Bombay Army, and to all the other officers, of both departments, under them, my acknowledgements are also due, for the manner in which their duties have been performed during this campaign.

Captain Alexander, commanding the 4th Bengal Local Horse, and Major Cunningham, commanding the Poona

Auxiliary Horse, with the men under their orders, have been of essential service to the Army in this campaign.

The arrangements made by Superintending Surgeons Kennedy and Atkinson, previous to the storming, for affording assistance and comfort to the wounded, met with my approval.

Major Parsons, the Deputy-Commissary-General in charge of the department in the field, has been unremitting in his attention to keep the troops supplied, although much difficulty is experienced, and he is occasionally thwarted by the nature of the country and its inhabitants.

I have, throughout this service, received the utmost assistance I could desire from Lieutenant-Colonel Macdonald, my officiating Military Secretary, and Deputy-Adjutant-General, H. M.'s Forces, Bombay, from Captain Powell, my Persian Interpreter, and the other officers of my personal staff. The nature of the country in which we are serving prevents the possibility of my sending a single staff officer to deliver this to your Lordship; otherwise, I should have asked my Aide-de-Camp, Lieutenant Keane, to proceed to Simla, to deliver this despatch into your hands, and to have afforded any further information that your Lordship could have desired.

The brilliant triumph we have obtained, the cool courage displayed, and the gallant bearing of the troops I have the honor to command, will have taught such a lesson to our enemies in the Affghan nation, as will make them hereafter respect the name of a British soldier.

Our loss is wonderfully small, considering the occasion; the casualties in killed and wounded amount to about 200.

The loss of the enemy is immense; we have already buried of their dead nearly 500, together with an immense number of horses.

I enclose a list of the killed, wounded, and missing. I am happy to say, that, although the wounds of some of the officers are severe, they are all doing well.

It is my intention, after selecting a garrison for this place, and establishing a general hospital, to continue my march to Cabool forthwith.

I have, &c.
(Signed) JOHN KEANE,
Lieutenant-General.

List of Killed, Wounded, and Missing, in the Army under the command of Lieutenant-General Sir John Keane, before Ghuznee, on the 21st July, 1839.

2d Troop Bengal Horse Artillery.—3 horses wounded.

3rd Bombay do. do.—2 rank and file, 2 horses wounded.

4th Bombay do. do.—1 horse killed.

2d Regiment Bengal Cavalry.—1 horse killed, 1 rank and file wounded.

4th Bengal Local Horse.—1 rank and file and 1 horse missing.

Her Majesty's 3rd Light Infantry.—1 rank and file killed.

16th Bengal Native Infantry.—1 captain wounded.

48th Bengal do. do. —1 lieutenant, and 2 rank and file wounded.

Total killed.—1 rank and file and 2 horses.

Total wounded.—1 captain, 1 lieutenant, 5 rank and file, and 6 horses.

Total missing.—1 rank and file, and 1 horse.

Names of Officers wounded.

Captain Graves, 16th Bengal Native Infantry,—severely.

Lieutenant Vanhomrigh, 48th Bengal N. I.,—slightly.

(Signed) R. MACDONALD, Lt.-Col.
Mily. Secy. and Deputy-Adjt.-Genl.
H. M.'s Forces, Bombay.

List of Killed, Wounded, and Missing, in the Army, under the Command of Lieut.-General Sir John Keane, K.C.B. and G. C. H., in the assault and capture of the fortress and citadel of Ghuznee, on the 23rd July, 1839.

General Staff.—1 colonel, 1 major wounded.

APPENDIX.—GHIZNI.

3d Troop Bombay Horse Artillery.—1 rank and file wounded.

4th do. do. do.—1 rank and file, and 1 horse wounded.

Bengal Engineers.—3 rank and file killed, 2 rank and file wounded, 1 rank and file missing.

Bombay Engineers.—1 lieutenant, 1 rank and file wounded.

2d Bengal Light Cavalry.—1 rank and file wounded.

1st Bombay Light Cavalry.—1 havildar killed, 5 rank and file, and 7 horses wounded.

Her Majesty's 2d Foot (or Queen's Royals).—4 rank and file killed, 2 captains, 4 lieutenants, 1 serjeant, and 26 rank and file wounded.

Her Majesty's 13th Light Infantry.—1 rank and file killed, 3 serjeants and 27 rank and file wounded.

Her Majesty's 17th Foot.—6 rank and file wounded.

Bengal European Regiment.—1 rank and file killed, 1 lieutenant-colonel, 1 major, 2 captains, 4 lieutenants, 1 ensign, 1 serjeant, 51 rank and file wounded.

16th Bengal Native Infantry.—1 havildar, 6 rank and file wounded.

35th do. do. —5 rank and file killed, 1 havildar, 8 rank and file wounded.

48th do. do. —2 havildars killed, 5 rank and file wounded.

Total killed.—3 serjeants or havildars, 14 rank and file.

Total wounded.—1 colonel, 1 lieutenant-colonel, 2 majors, 4 captains, 8 lieutenants, 2 ensigns, 7 serjeants or havildars, 140 rank and file, 8 horses.

Total missing.—1 rank and file.

Grand total on the 21st and 23rd of July, killed, wounded, and missing, 191 officers and men, and 15 horses.

(Signed) R. MACDONALD, Lt.-Col.
Mily. Secy. and Deputy-Adj.-Genl.
H. M.'s Forces, Bombay.

Names of Officers wounded.

General Staff.—Brigadier Sale, H. M.'s 13th Light Infantry, slightly; Major Parsons, Deputy-Commissary-Gen., slightly.

Bombay Engineers.—2d Lieutenant Marriott, slightly.

Her Majesty's 2d (or Queen's Royals).—Captain Raitt, slightly; Captain Robinson, severely; Lieutenant Yonge, do.; Lieutenant Stisted, slightly; Adjutant Simons, do.; Quarter-Master Hadley, do.

Bengal European Regiment.—Lieut.-Colonel Orchard, slightly; Major Warren, severely; Captain Hay, slightly; Captain Taylor, do.; Lieutenant Broadfoot, slightly; Lieutenant Haslewood, severely; Lieutenant Fagan, slightly; Lieutenant Magnay, do.; Ensign Jacob, do.

(Signed)   R. MACDONALD, Lt.-Col.
Mily. Secy. and Deputy-Adj.-Genl.
H. M.'s Forces, Bombay.
(True Copies.)
T. H. MADDOCK,
Offg. Secy. to Govt. of India, with the Govr.-Genl.

MEMORANDA *of the Engineers' operations before Ghuznee, in July*, 1839, *by Captains Thomson and Peat.*

The accounts of the Fortress of Ghuznee, received from those who had seen it, were such as to induce His Excellency the Commander-in-Chief to leave in Kandahar the very small battering train then with the Army, there being a scarcity of transport cattle. The place was described as very weak, and completely commanded from a range of hills to the north.

When we came before it, on the morning of the 21st July, we were very much surprised to find a high rampart, in good repair, built on a scarped mound, about 35 feet high, flanked by numerous towers, and surrounded by a fausse-braye and wet ditch. The irregular figure of the "enceinte" gave a good flanking fire, whilst the height of the citadel covered the interior from the commanding fire of the hills to the north, rendering it nugatory. In addition to this, the towers, at the angles, had been enlarged, screen walls had been built before the gates, the ditch cleared out and filled with water, stated to be unfordable, and an outwork built on the right bank of the river so as to command the bed of it.

The Garrison was variously stated from 3 to 4000 strong including 500 Cavalry, and from subsequent information we found that *it had not been overrated.*

On the approach of the Army, a fire of Artillery was opened from the body of the place, and of musketry from the neighbouring gardens. A detachment of Infantry cleared the latter, and the former was silenced for a short time by shrapnells from the Horse Artillery, but the fire from the new outwork on the bank of the river was in no way checked. A nearer view of the works was, however, obtained from the gardens which had been cleared. This was not at all satisfactory. The works were evidently much stronger than we had been led to expect, and such as our Army could not venture to attack in a regular manner. We had no battering train, and to besiege Ghuznee in form a much larger one would be required than the Army ever possessed. The great command of the parapets, from 60 to 70 feet, with the wet ditch, *were insurmountable obstacles to an attack, either by mining or escalading.*

It therefore became necessary to examine closely the whole " *Contour*" of the place, to discover if any other mode of attack could be adopted. The Engineers with an escort went round the works, approaching as near as they could find cover. The Garrison were on the alert, and kept up a hot and well-regulated fire upon the officers, whenever they were obliged to show themselves. However, by keeping the Infantry beyond musket range, and the Cavalry at a still greater distance, only one man was killed and another wounded; the former being hit by men sent out of the place to drive off the reconnoitring party.

The fortifications were found equally strong all round, the only tangible point observed being the Cabool gateway, which offered the following advantages for a " *Coup-de-main.*" The road to the gate was clear, the bridge over the ditch unbroken, there were good positions for the Artillery within 300 yards of the walls on both sides of the road, and we had information that the gateway was not built up, a reinforcement from Cabool being expected.

The result of this reconnoissance was a report to His Excellency the Commander-in-Chief that, if he decided upon the immediate attack of Ghuznee, the only feasible mode of proceeding, and the only one which held out a prospect of success, was a dash at the Cabool gateway, blowing the gate open by bags of powder.

His Excellency decided upon the attempt, the camp was moved that evening to the Cabool road, and the next morning, the 22d, Sir John Keane, in person reconnoitred the proposed point of attack, approved of the plan, and gave orders for its execution. Preparations were made accordingly, positions for the Artillery were carefully examined, which excited the jealousy of the Garrison, who opened a smart fire upon the party.

It was arranged that an explosion party, consisting of three officers of Engineers, Captain Peat, Lieutenants Durand and Mc. Leod, 3 serjeants, and 18 men of the Sappers, in working dresses, carrying 300 lbs. of powder, in 12 sand-bags, with a hose 72 feet long, should be ready to move down to the gateway at daybreak.

At midnight the first battery left camp, followed by the other four, at intervals of half-an-hour. Those to the right of the road were conducted to their positions by Lieutenant Stuart, those to the left by Lieutenant Anderson. The ground for the guns was prepared by the Sappers and Pioneers, taking advantage of the irregularities of the ground to the right, and of some old garden walls to the left.

The Artillery was all in position and ready by 3 A. M. of the 23rd, and shortly after, at the first dawn, the party under Captain Peat moved down to the gateway, accompanied by six men of H. M.'s 13th Light Infantry, without their belts, and supported by a detachment of the same Regiment, which extended to the right and left of the road, when they arrived at the ditch, taking advantage of what cover they could find, and endeavouring to keep down the fire from the ramparts, which became heavy on the approach of the party, though it had been remarkably slack during the previous operations. Blue lights were shown, which rendered surrounding objects distinctly visible; but, luckily, they were burned on the top of the parapet, instead of being thrown into the passage below.

The explosion party marched steadily on, headed by Lieut. Durand; the powder was placed, the hose laid, the train fired, and the carrying party had retired to tolerable cover in less than two minutes. The Artillery opened when the blue lights appeared, and the musketry from the covering party at the same time. So quickly was the operation performed, and so little was the enemy aware of the nature of it, that not a man of the party was hurt.

As soon as the explosion took place, Captain Peat, although hurt by the concussion, his anxiety preventing him from keeping sufficiently under cover, ran up to the gate, accompanied by a small party of H. M.'s 13th Light Infantry, and ascertained that it was completely destroyed. There was some delay in getting a bugler to sound at the advance the signal agreed on for the assaulting column to push on, and this was the only mistake in the operation.

The assaulting column, consisting of 4 European Regiments (H. M.'s 2nd Regiment, Bengal European Regiment, H. M.'s 13th L. I. and H. M.'s 12th Regiment), commanded by Brigadier Sale, the advance under Lieutenant-Colonel Dennie, accompanied by Lieutenant Stuart, Engineers, moved steadily through the gateway, through a passage inside the gateway, in a domed building, which the opening on one side rendered everything very obscure, and rendered it difficult to find the outlet into the town. They met with little opposition; but a party of the enemy, seeing a peak in the column, owing to the difficulty in scrambling over the rubbish in the gateway, made a rush, sword in hand, and cut down a good many men, wounding the Brigadier and several other officers. These swordsmen were repulsed, and there was no more regular opposition; the surprise and alarm of the

Governor and Sirdars being so great, when they saw the column occupying the open space inside the gate, and firing upon them, that they fled, accompanied by their men, even the Garrison of the citadel following their example. Parties of the Affghans took refuge in the houses, firing on the column as it made its way through the streets, and a good deal of desultory fighting took place in consequence. As soon as daylight showed that the citadel had been abandoned by the enemy, the whole of the works were in our possession before 5 A.M.

We lost 17 men, 6 Europeans and 11 Natives, killed;—18 Officers and 117 Europeans and 30 Natives wounded; total, 182. Of the Affghans more than 514 were killed in the town, that number of bodies having been buried, and about 100 outside by the Cavalry; 1600 prisoners were taken, but I have no means of estimating the number of wounded.

There were nine guns of different calibres found in the place, a large quantity of good powder, considerable stores of shot lead, &c. &c., and a large supply of atta and other provisions.

(Signed)   GEO. THOMSON, Capt. Engrs.,
Chief Engr. Army of the Indus.

During the reconnoissance the wall pieces were particularly troublesome. This weapon is almost unknown in our service, but it is a very efficient one, especially in the defence of works, and its use should not be neglected. Every fortified post should be supplied with a proportion of them, and a certain number of men in every Regiment practised in firing them.

The charge recommended by Col. Pasley, for blowing open gates is from 60 to 120 lbs., and this is, doubtless, sufficient in ordinary cases; but, in this instance, we were apprehensive that the enemy might have taken alarm at our being so much on that side of the place, and in consequence partially or wholly built up the gateway. It was afterwards found that some attempts of the kind had been made, by propping up the gate with beams.

The charge was so heavy, that it not only destroyed the gate, but brought down a considerable portion of the roof of the square building in which it was placed, which proved a very considerable obstacle to the assaulting column; and the concussion acted as far as the tower A, under which an officer's party of H. M.'s 13th Regt. were standing at the time, but without occasioning any casualties. In cases of this nature, it is, of course, the first object to guard against any chance of failure; and it is impossible even now to say how much the charge might have been reduced with safety.

The enemy appeared so much on the alert, and the faussebraye was so much in advance of the gate that we never contemplated being able to effect our object by surprise. The only question was, whether it ought to be done by day or night. It was argued, in favour of the former, that the Artillery would be able to make so much more correct practice, that the defences would be in a considerable degree destroyed, and the fire so completely kept under as to enable the explosion party to advance with but little loss, and with the advantage of being able to see exactly what they were about. Captain Thomson, however, adhered to the latter, and we were afterwards convinced it was the most judicious plan; for, although the fire of the Artillery was necessarily more general than it would have been in daylight, still it was so well directed as to take up a good deal of the attention of the besieged, and draw upon their batteries a portion of the fire which in daylight would have been thrown upon the explosion party and assaulting columns. It would also, even in daylight, have been difficult, with our light Artillery, to have kept down the fire so completely but that a few matchlock men might have kept their position near the gateway, and in that narrow space a smart fire from a few pieces might have obliged the party to retire. The obscurity of the night, to say nothing of the confusion which it must occasion among undisciplined troops, is certainly the best protection to a body of men engaged in an enterprise of this nature. Blue lights certainly render objects distinctly visible, but their light is glaring and uncertain, especially to men firing through loop-holes.

The party of H. M.'s 13th consisted of 18 officers, 28 serjeants, 7 buglers, 276 rank and file.

It was made of this strength not only to keep up a heavy fire upon the parapets, and thereby divert attention from the party at the gateway, but also because we were not aware whether the fausse-braye was occupied or not, and as it extends so much in advance as to take the gate completely in reverse, it would have been necessary, had a fire opened from it, to have carried it by assault before the party with the bags could have advanced. The party with Lieut. Durand was accompanied by 6 men of the 13th, without their belts, the better to secure them from observation, to protect them from any sortie that might be made from the postern B of the fausse-braye on the right, or even from the gate itself, while another party under an officer, Lieutenant Jennings, accompanied me as far as the tower A, so as to check any attempts that might have been made from the fausse-braye on the left, and at the same time keeping up a fire on such of the enemy as showed their heads above the parapet: of this party one man was killed and a few wounded.

Nothing could have been more gallant than the conduct of Lieuts. Durand and Mc.Leod, and the men under their command, or more efficient than the manner in which they executed their duty.

The powder being in sand-bags, of a very coarse open texture, a long hose and portfire was thought to be the safest method of firing it. The end of the hose fortunately just reached the small postern B. The casualties during this operation were much fewer than was expected, being in all 1 private killed, 2 serjeants and 23 rank and file wounded.

The heaviest fire was certainly outside the bridge; for the enemy, near the gateway, being marked whenever they attempted to show their heads above the parapet, were obliged to confine themselves to the loop-holes, the range from which is very uncertain and limited against men moving about.

A high loop-holed wall, although imposing in appearance, is a profile but ill adapted to resist attacks of this nature.

The enemy were perfectly aware that we were in the gateway, but appeared to have no idea of the nature of our operations. Had they been so, they might easily have rendered it impossible to place the powder-bags, by throwing over blue lights of which they had a large quantity in store. The powder pots and other fire-works, so much used by the natives of Hindoostan, would certainly have rendered the confined space leading to the gate much too hot for such an operation; but the ignorance of the besieged was known and calculated upon, the result shews how justly.

Their attempts at resistance were confined to the fire from the loop-holes, and throwing over large pieces of earth, some of which appeared to be intended to knock off the portfire.

I on this occasion received an excellent lesson on the necessity of not allowing preconceived opinions to lead to any carelessness, in accurately ascertaining the result of any operation of this nature. The gateway appeared, from what I had seen from the hills to the north, to lead straight into the town; and, on running in to examine it after the explosion, I was so much impressed with this idea, and so much convinced of the probability of the gateway having been blocked up during the day, that I was led to believe that it had actually been done, from seeing, in front of the gate that had been destroyed, the outline of an arch filled up with brick masonry. The true entrance turned to the right, and would have been discovered by advancing a few paces, and that in perfect safety, for the interior was secure from all fire. Lieutenant Durand, on first going up, saw, from through the chinks of the gate, that there was a light, and a guard immediately behind it; and, from that circumstance, was convinced that no interior obstacles of importance existed.

My mistake, therefore, was luckily immediately corrected, without any bad consequence resulting,

A party of Sappers, with felling axes, and commanded by Lieutenant Wemyss, and two scaling ladders, in charge of Lieutenant Pigan, accompanied the assaulting column.

Of 10 Engineer officers, engaged in this attack, only one, Lieutenant Marriot, was slightly wounded. Captain Thomson, however, had a very narrow escape, having been thrown down by a rush of some swordsmen into the gateway, and nearly sabred while upon the ground.

(Signed)   A. G. PEAT, Captain,
Bombay Engineers.

No. 4.

CABUL.

NOTIFICATION BY THE GOVERNOR-GENERAL.

Secret Department.

Simla, the 26th August, 1839.

The Governor-General of India publishes for general information the subjoined copy and extracts of despatches from His Excellency the Commander-in-Chief of the Army of the Indus, and from the Envoy and Minister at the Court of His Majesty Shah Shooja ool Moolk, announcing the triumphant entry of the Shah into Cabool on the 7th instant.

In issuing this notification, the Governor-General cannot omit the opportunity of offering to the officers and men composing the Army of the Indus, and to the distinguished leader, by whom they have been commanded, the cordial congratulations of the Government upon the happy result of a campaign, which, on the sole occasion when resistance was opposed to them, has been gloriously marked by victory, and in all the many difficulties of which the character of a British Army for gallantry, good conduct, and discipline, has been nobly maintained.

A salute of 21 guns will be fired, on the receipt of this intelligence, at all the principal Stations of the Army in the three Presidencies.

By order of the Right Honorable the Governor-General of India.

T. H. MADDOCK,
Offg. Secy. to the Govt. of India, with the Gov.-Genl.

To the Right Honorable Lord Auckland, G. C. B.
&c. &c. &c.

My Lord,—We have the honor to acquaint your Lordship, that the Army marched from Ghuznee *en route* to Cabool, in two columns, on the 30th and 31st ultimo, His Majesty Shah Shooja ool Moolk, with his own troops, forming part of the 2d column.

On the arrival of the Commander-in-Chief with the first column at Hyder Khail on the 1st instant, information reached him, and the same reached the Envoy and Minister at Huft Assaya, that Dost Mahommed, with his army and artillery, were advancing from Cabool, and would probably take up a position at Urghundee or Midan, (the former twenty-four, the latter thirty-six miles from Cabool). Upon this it was arranged that His Majesty, with the 2nd column, under Major-General Willshire, should join the 1st column here, and advance together to attack Dost Mahommed, whose son, Mahommed Akhbur, had been recalled from Jellalabad, with the troops guarding the Khyber Pass, and had formed a junction with his father, their joint forces, according to our information, amounting to about 13,000 men.

Every arrangement was made for the King and the Army marching in a body from here to-morrow ; but in the course of the night, messengers arrived, and since (this morning), a great many Chiefs and their followers, announcing the dissolution of Dost Mahommed's army, by the refusal of the greater part to advance against us with him, and that he had, in consequence, fled with a party of 300 horsemen, in the direction of Bamian, leaving his guns behind him in position as they were placed at Urghundee.

His Majesty Shah Shooja has sent forward a confidential officer, with whom has been associated Major Cureton, of Her Majesty's 16th Lancers, taking with him a party of 200 men, and an officer of Artillery, to proceed direct to take possession of those guns, and, afterwards, such other guns and public stores as may be found in

Cabool and the Balla Hissar, in the name of, and for His Majesty Shah Shooja ool Moolk, and the King's order will be carried by his own officer with this party, for preserving the tranquillity of the city of Cabool.

A strong party has been detached in pursuit of Dost Mahommed, under some of our most active officers. We continue our march upon Cabool to-morrow. and will reach it on the third day.

We have, &c.,
(Signed) JOHN KEANE, Lt.-Genl.
Commander-in-Chief.
(Signed) W. H. MACNAGHTEN,
Envoy and Minister.

Head Quarters, Camp Shikarbad, 3d August, 1839.
T. H. MADDOCK,
Offg. Secy. to the Govt. of India, with the Gov.-Genl.

Extract of a Letter, from His Excellency Lieut.-General Sir John Keane, K. C. B. and G. C. H., dated Head Quarters, Camp Cabool, 8th August, 1839.

"It gives me infinite pleasure to be able to address my despatch to your Lordship from the capital, the vicinity of which, His Majesty Shah Shooja ool Moolk, and the Army under my command, reached the day before yesterday. The King entered his capital yesterday afternoon, accompanied by the British Envoy and Minister, and the gentlemen of the mission, and by myself, the Generals and Staff officers of this Army, and escorted by a squadron of Her Majesty's 4th Light Dragoons, and one of Her Majesty's 16th Lancers, with Captain Martin's Troop of Horse Artillery. His Majesty had expressed a wish that British troops should be present on the occasion, and a very small party only of his own Hindostanee and Affghan troops. After the animating scene of traversing the streets and reaching the palace in the Balla Hissar, a royal salute was fired, and an additional salvo in the Affghan style, from small guns resembling wall pieces, named jingalls, and carried on camels. We heartily congratulated His Majesty on being in possession of the throne and kingdom of his ancestors, and upon the overthrow of his enemies; and, after taking leave of His Majesty, we returned to our camp.

"I trust we have thus accomplished all the objects which your Lordship had in contemplation, when you planned and formed the Army of the Indus, and the expedition into Affghanistan.

"The conduct of the Army, both European and Native, which your Lordship did me the honour to place under my orders, has been admirable throughout; and, notwithstanding the severe marching and privations they have gone through, their appearance and discipline have suffered nothing, and the opportunity afforded them at Ghuznee of meeting and conquering their enemy, has added greatly to their good spirits.

"The joint despatch addressed by Mr. Macnaghten and myself to your Lordship on the 3rd instant, from Shikarbad, will have informed you that, at the moment we had made every preparation to attack (on the following day) Dost Mahommed Khan, in his position at Urghundee, where, after his son Mahommed Ahkbar had joined him from Jellalabad, he had an army amounting to 13,000 men, well armed and appointed, and 30 pieces of artillery, we suddenly learnt that he abandoned them all, and fled with a party of horsemen on the road to Bamian, leaving his guns in position as he had placed them to receive our attack.

"It appears that a great part of his army, which was hourly becoming disorganized, refused to stand by him in the position, to receive our attack, and that it soon became in a state of dissolution. The great bulk immediately came over to Shah Shooja, tendering their allegiance, and I believe His Majesty will take most of them into his pay.

"It seems that the news of the quick and determined manner in which we took their stronghold, Ghuznee, had such an effect upon the population of Cabool, and perhaps also upon the enemy's army, that Dost Mahommed, from that moment, began to lose hope of retaining his rule for even a short time longer, and sent off his family and valuable property towards Bamian, but marched out of Cabool with his army and artillery, keeping a bold front towards us until the evening of the 2d, when all his hopes were at an end by a division in his own camp, and one part of his army abandoning him. So precipitate was his flight, that he left in position his guns, with their ammunition and waggons, and the greater part of their cattle by which they were drawn. Major Cureton, of Her Majesty's 16th Lancers, with his party of 200 men, pushed forward on the 3d, and took possession of those guns, &c. There were 23 brass guns in position and loaded, two more at a little distance, which they attempted to take away, and, since then, three more, abandoned still farther off on the Bamian road—thus, leaving in our possession 28 pieces of cannon, with all the material belonging to them, which are now handed over to Shah Shooja ool Moolk."

T. H. MADDOCK,
Offg. Secy. to Govt. of India, with the Gov.-Genl.

Extract of a Letter from W. H. Macnaghten, Esq., Envoy and Minister to the Court of Shah Shooja ool Moolk, dated Cabool, 8th August, 1839.

"By a letter signed jointly by His Excellency Lieutenant-General Sir John Keane and myself, dated the 3d instant, the Right Honorable the Governor-General was apprised of the flight of Dost Mahommed Khan.

"The Ex-Chief was not accompanied by any person of consequence, and his followers are said to have been reduced to below the number of one hundred, on the day of his departure. In the progress of Shah Shooja ool Moolk towards Cabul, His Majesty was joined by every person of rank and influence in the country, and he made his triumphal entry into the city, on the evening of the 7th inst. His Majesty has taken up his residence in the Balla Hissar, where he has required the British mission to remain for the present.

T. H. MADDOCK,
Offg. Secy. to the Govt. of India with the Gov.-Genl.

No. 5

GENERAL ORDERS

BY THE RIGHT HONOURABLE THE GOVERNOR-GENERAL OF
INDIA, ON THE BREAKING UP OF THE ARMY OF THE INDUS.

Secret Department.

Camp Paniput, the 18*th November,* 1839.

Intelligence was this day received of the arrival, within the Peshawur Territory, of His Excellency Lieutenant-General Sir John Keane, G. C. B. and G. C. H., Commander-in-Chief of the Army of the Indus, with a portion of that Force on its return to the British Provinces. The Military operations under the direction of His Excellency, having now been brought to a close, the Right Hon'ble the Governor-General has, on the part of the Government of India, to acquit himself of the gratifying duty of offering publicly his warmest thanks to His Excellency and to the Officers and Men, who have served under his command, for the soldier-like spirit and conduct of all ranks throughout the late Campaign, and he again cordially congratulates them on the attainment of the great objects of national security and honour for which the expedition was undertaken.

The plans of aggression by which the British Empire in India was dangerously threatened, have, under Providence, been arrested. The Chiefs of Cabool, and Candahar, who had joined in hostile designs against us, have been deprived of power, and the Territories which they ruled have been restored to the Government of a friendly Monarch. The Ameers of Scinde have acknowledged the supremacy of the British Government, and ranged themselves under its protection. Their country will now be an outwork of defence, and the navigation of the Indus within their dominions, exempt from all duties, has been opened to commercial enterprise. With the allied Government of the Sikhs, the closest harmony has been maintained—and on the side of Herat, the British Alliance has been courted, and a good understanding, with a view to common safety, has been established with that power.

For these important results, the Governor-General is proud to express the acknowledgment of the Government to the Army of the Indus, which alike by its valor,—its discipline and cheerfulness under hardships and privations,—and its conciliatory conduct to the inhabitants of the countries through which it passed, has earned respect for the British name, and has confirmed in Central Asia a just impression of British energy and resources.

The Native and European Soldier have vied with each other in effort and endurance. A march of extraordinary length, through difficult and untried countries, has been within a few months successfully accomplished. And in the capture of the one stronghold, where resistance was attempted, a trophy of victory has been won which will add a fresh lustre to the reputation of the Armies of India.

To Lieutenant-General Sir John Keane, the Commander-in-Chief of the Army, the Governor-General would particularly declare his thanks for his direction of these honourable achievements. He would especially acknowledge the marked forbearance, and just appreciation of the views of the Government, which guided His Excellency in his intercourse with the Ameers of Scinde. He feels the Government to be under the deepest obligations to His Excellency for the unshaken firmness of purpose with which, throughout the whole course of the operations, obstacles and discouragements were disregarded, and the prescribed objects of policy were pursued. And above all, he would warmly applaud the decisive judgment, with which the attack upon the fortress of Ghuznee was planned and its capture effected. Nor would he omit to remark upon that spirit of perfect co-opera-

with which His Excellency gave all support to the Political Authorities with whom he was associated. Mr. Macnaghten, the Envoy and Minister at the Court of Shah Shooja-ool-Moolk, and Colonel Pottinger, the Resident in Scinde, have been chiefly enabled by the cordial good understanding which has throughout subsisted between them and His Excellency to render the important services by which they have entitled themselves to the high approbation of the Government—and His Lordship has much pleasure in noticing the feeling of satisfaction with which His Excellency regarded the valuable services of Lieutenant-Colonel Sir Alexander Burnes, who was politically attached to him in the advance upon Ghuznee.

The Governor-General would follow His Excellency the Commander-in-Chief in acknowledging the manner in which Major-General Sir Willoughby Cotton, K. C. B. and K. C. H. exercised his Command of the Bengal Division throughout the Campaign and supported the honour of his Country on the 23rd of July, and his Lordship would also offer the thanks of the Government to Major-General Willshire, C B., Commanding the 2nd Infantry Division, to Major-General Thackwell, C. B. and K. H., Commanding the Bengal Division, to Brigadier Roberts, Commanding the 4th Infantry Brigade, to Brigadier Stevenson, Commanding the Artillery of the Army, to Brigadier Scott, Commanding the Bombay Cavalry Brigade, and to Brigadier Persse, upon whom, on the lamented death of the late Brigadier Arnold, devolved the command of the Bengal Cavalry Brigade, as well as to the Commandants of Corps and Detachments, with the Officers and men under their respective Commands, and to the Officers at the head of the several departments, with all of whom His Excellency the Commander-in-Chief has expressed his high satisfaction.

To Brigadier Sale, C. B. already honourably distinguished in the annals of Indian warfare, who commanded the storming party at Ghuznee, to Lieut. Colonel Dennie, C. B. who led the advance on the same occasion, and to Captain George Thomson, of the Bengal Engineers, whose services in the capture of that fortress have been noticed in marked terms of commendation by His Excellency the Commander-in-Chief, and to Captain Peat of the Bombay Engineers, and to Lieutenants Durand and Macleod, of the Bengal Engineers, and the other officers and men of the Bengal and Bombay Engineers under their command, the Governor-General would especially tender the expression of his admiration of the gallantry and science which they respectively displayed in the execution of the important duties confided to them in that memorable operation.

In testimony of the services of the Army of the Indus, the Governor-General is pleased to resolve, that all the corps, European and Native, in the service of the East India Company, which proceeded beyond the Bolan Pass, shall have on their regimental colours the word "Affghanistan," and such of them as were employed in the reduction of the fortress of that name, the word "Ghuznee," in addition.

In behalf of the Queen's Regiments, the Governor-General will recommend to her Majesty, through the proper channel, that the same distinction may be granted to them.

The Governor-General would here notice with approbation the praiseworthy conduct, during this expedition, of the officers and men attached to the disciplined force of His Majesty Shah Shooja-ool-Moolk. This force was newly raised, and opportunities had not been afforded for its perfect organization and instruction. But it shared honourably in the labours and difficulties of the Campaign, and it had the good fortune in repelling an attack made by the enemy in force, on the day prior to the storming of Ghuznee, to be enabled to give promise of the excellent service which may hereafter be expected from it.

His Lordship has also much satisfaction in adding that the best acknowledgments of the Government are due to Lieut. Colonel Wade, who was employed upon the Peshawur Frontier, and who, gallantly supported by the officers and men of all ranks under him, and seconded by the cordial aid of the Sikh Government—an aid, the more honourable, because rendered at a painful crisis of its affairs,—opened the Khyber Pass, and overthrew the authority of the enemy at that quarter, at the moment when the advance of the forces of the Shahzadah Timoor could most conduce to the success of the general operation.

By command of the Right Honourable the Governor-General of India.

T. H. MADDOCK,
Offg. Secy. to the Govt. of India, with the Gov. Genl.

Camp Paniput, 18*th November,* 1839.

The Right Hon'ble the Governor-General, having taken into consideration the heavy losses and expences incurred by the Commissioned Officers and European Troops serving with the Army of the Indus, and being desirous also to mark his admiration of the intrepidity and soldier-like bearing evinced by all portions of that Army, European and Native, during the recent Campaign in Affghanistan, has been pleased to resolve that a donation of six months full or field Batta shall be granted to the Officers and fighting Men of every rank attached to the Army, who advanced beyond the Bolan Pass.

The Hon' ble the President in Council is requested to issue such Subsidiary Orders as may be necessary for giving effect to His Lordship's resolution.

J. STUART, Lieutenant-Colonel.
Secy. to the Govt. of India Mily. Dept.
with the Governor-General.

No. 6.

KHELAT.

Secret Department.

Camp Deothanee, 4th December, 1839.

The many outrages and murders committed, in attacks on the followers of the Army of the Indus, by the plundering tribes in the neighbourhood of the Bolan Pass, at the instigation of their Chief, Meer Mehrab Khan of Khelat, at a time when he was professing friendship for the British Government, and negotiating a Treaty with its representatives, having compelled the Government to direct a detachment of the Army to proceed to Khelat, for the exaction of retribution from that Chieftain, and for the execution of such arrangements as would establish future security in that quarter, a Force under the orders of Major-General Willshire, C. B. was employed on this service, and the Right Honorable the Governor-General of India having this day received that officer's report of the successful accomplishment of the objects entrusted to him, has been pleased to direct that the following copy of the despatch dated 14th ultimo, be published for general information.

The Right Honorable the General is happy to avail himself of this opportunity to record his high admiration of the signal gallantry and spirit of the troops engaged on this occasion, and offers, on the part of the Government, his best thanks to Major-General Willshire, and to the officers and men who served under him.

T. H. MADDOCK,
Offg. Secy. to Govt. of India,
with the Govr.-Genl.

To the Right Hon. Lord Auckland, G. C. B.
Governor-General of India, &c. &c. &c.

My Lord,—In obedience to the joint instructions furnished me by His Excellency the Commander-in-Chief of the Army of the Indus, and the Envoy and Minister to His Majesty Shah Shooja, under date Cabool, the 17th September, 1839, deputing to me the duty of deposing Mehrab Khan of Khelat, in consequence of the avowed hostility of that Chief to the British nation during the present Campaign, I have the honor to report that, on my arrival at Quetta, on the 31st ultimo, I communicated with Captain Bean, the Political Agent in Shawl, and arranged with him the best means of giving effect to the orders I had received.

<small>Two Guns Bombay Horse Artillery.
Four Guns Shah's Artillery.
Two Ressalas Local Horse.
Queen's Royals.
H. M.'s 17th Regt.
31st Bengal N. I.
Bombay Engineers.</small>
In consequence of the want of public carriage, and the limited quantity of Commissariat supplies at Quetta, as well as the reported want of forage on the route to Khelat, I was obliged to despatch to Cutch Gandava the whole of the Cavalry, and the greater portion of the Artillery, taking with me only the Troops noted in the margin, leaving Quetta on the 3rd inst.

During the march the communications received from Mehrab Khan were so far from acceding to the terms offered, that he threatened resistance if the Troops approached his capital. I therefore proceeded and arrived at the village of Giranee, within 8 miles of Khelat, on the 12th instant.

Marching from hence the following morning, a body of horse were perceived on the right of the road, which commenced firing on the advanced guard, commanded by Major Pennycuick, H. M.'s 17th Regiment, as the column advanced; and skirmishing between them continued until we came in sight of Khelat, rather less than a mile distance.

I now discovered that three heights on the N. W. face of the fort, and parallel to the North, were covered with Infantry, with five guns in position, protected by small parapet walls.

Captain Peat, Chief Engineer, immediately reconnoitred, and having reported that nothing could be done until those heights were in our possession, I decided at once on storming them simultaneously, and, if practicable, entering the fort with the fugitives, as the gate in the Northern face was occasionally opened to keep up the communication between the fort and the heights.

To effect this object, I detached a company from each of the European Regiments from the advanced guard, with Major Pennycuick, H. M.'s 17th Regiment, for the purpose of occupying the gardens and enclosures to the North-East of the town, and two more companies in the plain, midway between them and the column; at the same time, I ordered three columns of attack to be formed, composed of four companies from each corps, under their respective commanding officers, Major Carruthers, of the Queen's, Lieut.-Colonel Croker, H. M.'s 17th Regiment, and Major Western, 31st Bengal N. I., the whole under the command of Brigadier Baumgardt; the remainder of the Regiments forming three columns of reserve, under my own direction, to move in support.

A hill being allotted to each column, Brigadier Stevenson commanding the Artillery, moved quickly forward in front, towards the base of the heights, and, when within the required range, opened a fire upon the Infantry and guns, under cover of which the columns moved steadily on, and commenced the ascent, for the purpose of carrying the heights exposed to the fire of the enemy's guns, which had commenced while the columns of attack were forming.

Before the columns reached their respective summits of the hills, the enemy, overpowered by the superior and well-directed fire of our Artillery, had abandoned them, attempting to carry off their guns, but which they were unable to do; at this moment it appearing to me the opportunity offered for the troops to get in with the fugitives, and, if possible, gain possession of the gate of the fortress, I despatched orders to the Queen's Royal and H. M.'s 17th Regiment, to make a rush from the heights for that purpose, following myself to the summit of the nearest to observe the result; at this moment, the four companies on my left, which had been detached to the gardens and plains, seeing the chance that offered of entering the fort, moved rapidly forward from their respective points towards the gateway, under a heavy and well-directed fire from the walls of the fort and citadel, which were thronged by the enemy.

The gate having been closed before the troops moving towards it could effect the desired object, and the Garrison strengthened by the enemy driven from the heights, they were compelled to cover themselves, as far as practicable, behind some walls and ruined buildings to the right and left of it, while Brigadier Stevenson, having ascended the heights with the Artillery, opened two guns, under the command of Lieutenant Foster, Bombay Horse Artillery, upon the defences above its gates and vicinity, while the fire of two others, commanded by Lieutenant Cowper, Shah's Artillery, was directed against the gate itself, the remaining two, with Lieutenant Creed, being sent round to the road on the left, leading direct up to the gate, and when within two hundred yards, commenced a fire for the purpose of blowing it open; and, after a few rounds, they succeeded in knocking in one-half of it; on observing this, I rode down the hill towards the gate, pointing to it, thereby announcing to the troops it was open; they instantly rose from their cover, and rushed in; those under the command of Major Pennycuick, being the nearest, were the first to gain the gate, headed by that officer; the whole of the storming column from the three Regiments rapidly following, and gaining an entrance as quickly as it was possible to do so, under a heavy fire from the works and from the interior, the enemy making a most gallant and determined resistance, disputing every inch of ground up to the walls of the inner citadel.

At this time I directed the reserve columns to be brought near the gate, and detached one company of the 17th Regt., under Captain Darby, to the Western side of the fort, followed by a portion of the 31st Bengal Native Infantry, commanded by Major Western, conducted by Capt. Outram, acting as my extra Aide-de-Camp, for the purpose of securing the heights under which the Southern angle is situated, and intercepting any of the Garrison escaping from that side. Having driven off the enemy from the heights above, the united detachments then descended to the gate of the fort below, and forced it open before the Garrison (who closed it as they saw the troops approach) had time to secure it.

When the party was detached by the Western face, I also sent two companies from the reserve of the 17th, under Major Dithon, and two guns of the Shah's Artillery, under the command of Lieutenant Creed, Bombay Artillery, by the Eastern to the Southern face, for the purpose of blowing open the gate above alluded to, had it been necessary, as well as the gate of the inner citadel, the Infantry joining the other detachments making their way through the town, in the direction of the citadel.

After some delay, the troops that held possession of the town at length succeeded in forcing an entrance into the citadel, where a desperate resistance was made by Mehrab Khan, at the head of his people, he himself, with many of his Chiefs, being killed sword in hand; several others, however, kept up a fire upon our troops from detached buildings difficult of access, and it was not until late in the afternoon that those who survived were induced to give themselves up on a promise of their lives being spared.

From every account I have reason to believe the Garrison consisted of upwards of 2,000 fighting men, and that the son of Mehrab Khan had been expected to join him from Nowsky, with a further reinforcement. The enclosed return will show the strength of the force under my command present at the capture.

The defences of the fort, as in the case of Ghuznee, far exceeded in strength what I had been led to suppose from previous report, and the towering height of the inner citadel was most formidable, both in appearance and reality.

I lament to say, that the loss of killed and wounded on our side has been severe, as will be seen by the accompanying return, that on the part of the enemy must have been great, but the exact number I have not been able to ascertain. Several hundreds of prisoners were taken, from whom the Political Agent has selected those he considers it necessary for the present to retain in confinement; the remainder have been liberated.

It is quite impossible for me sufficiently to express my admiration of the gallant and steady conduct of the officers and men upon the occasion, but the fact of less than an hour having elapsed from the formation of the columns for the attack to the period of the troops being within the fort, and that performed in the open day, and in the face of an enemy so very superior in number, and so perfectly prepared for resistance, will, I trust, convince your Lordship how deserving the officers and troops are of my warmest thanks, and of the highest praise that can be bestowed.

To Brigadier Baumgardt, commanding the storming column, my best thanks are due, and he reports that Capt. Wyllie, Acting Asst.-Adjt.-Genl., and Capt. Gilland, his Aides-de-Camp, ably assisted him, and zealously performed their duties; also to Brigr. Stevenson, commanding the Artillery, Lieutenants Forster and Cowper respectively, in charge of the Bombay and Shah's Artillery, I feel greatly indebted for the steady and scientific manner in which the service of dislodging the enemy from the heights, and afterwards effecting an entrance into the fort, was performed. The Brigadier has brought to my notice the assistance he received from Captain Coghlan his Brigade-Major, Lieut. Woosnam, his Aide-de-Camp, and Lieut. Creed, when in battery yesterday.

To Lieut.-Col. Croker, commanding H. M.'s 17th Regt., Major Carruthers, commanding the Queen's Royals, Major Western, commanding the Bengal 31st N. I., I feel highly indebted for the manner in which they conducted their respective columns to the attack of the heights, and afterwards to the assault of the fort, as well as to Major Pennycuick, of the 17th, who led the advanced guard companies to the same point.

To Captain Peat, Chief Engineer, and to the officers and

men of the Engineer corps my acknowledgements are due—to Major Neil Campbell, Acting Quarter-Master-General of the Bombay Army, to Captain Hagart, Acting Deputy-Adjutant-General, and to Lieutenant Ramsay, Acting Assistant-Quarter-Master-General, my best thanks are due for the able assistance afforded me by their services.

It is with much pleasure I take this opportunity of acknowledging my obligations to Major Campbell for relieving me from the necessity of returning by the route by which the Army advanced to Cabool, which being entirely exhausted, must have subjected the troops to great privations and the horses to absolute starvation; the Quarter-Master-General took upon himself the responsibility of leading my column through the heart of Ghiljee and Koohul countries, never hitherto traversed by Europeans, by which our route was considerably shortened, a sufficiency obtained, and great additions made to our geographical knowledge of the country, besides great political advantages obtained in peaceably settling those districts.

From my Aides-de-Camp, Captain Robinson, and Lieutenant Halkett, as well as from Captain Outram, who volunteered his services on my personal Staff, I received the utmost assistance, and to the latter officer I feel greatly indebted for the zeal and ability with which he has performed various duties that I have required of him, upon other occasions as well as the present.

It is with much satisfaction I am able to state that the utmost cordiality has existed between the Political Authorities and myself, and to acknowledge the great assistance I have derived from Captain Bean in obtaining supplies.

After allowing time to make the necessary arrangements for continuing in my march, I shall descend into Cutch Gundava by the Moona Pass, having received a favourable report of the practicability of taking guns that way.

I have deputed Captain Outram to take a duplicate of the despatch to the Honorable the Governor of Bombay by the direct route from hence to Sonmeanee Bunder, the practicability or otherwise of which for the passage of troops, I consider it an object of importance to ascertain.

I have, &c.
(Signed) T. WILLSHIRE, Major-General,
Commanding Bombay Column, Army of the Indus.

APPENDIX.—KHELAT.

Return of casualties in the Army under the command of Major-General Willshire, C. B., employed at the storming of Khelat, on the 13th November, 1839.

CORPS.	KILLED.				WOUNDED.									Total killed & wounded	Killed	Wounded	HORSE
	Lieutenants	Subedors	Rank and File	Total	Captains	Lieutenants	Ensigns	Adjutants	Jemadars	Serjeants	Drummers	Rank and File	Regt. Bheesties	Total			
Detachment 3d Troop Horse Artillery ..																	
1st Troop Cabool Artillery	0	0	0	0	0	0	0	0	0	None 0	2	0		2	2	0	6
Gun Lascars attd. to do.	0	0	0	0	0	0	0	0	0	0	0	1	0	1	1	0	0
H. M.'s 2d or Queen's Royal Regiment .	1	0	21	22	2	2	0	1	0	2	0	40	0	47	69	0	1
H M.'s 17th Regiment	0	0	6	6	1	0	0	0	0	3	0	29	0	33	39	0	0
31st Regt. Bengal N. I.	0	1	2	3	1	0	1	0	2	2	1	14	1	22	25	0	0
Sappers, Miners, and Pioneers	0	0	0	0	0	0	0	0	1	0	0	0		1	1	0	0
2 Resillas of the 4th Bengal Local Horse.	0	0	0	0	0	0	0	0	0	0	1	0		1	1	0	0
Total ...	1	1	29	34	4	2	1	1	2	8	1	87	1	107	138	0	7

Missing, None.

Names of Officers killed and wounded.

KILLED.   REMARKS.
Corps.   Rank and Names.

H. M.'s 2d or Queen's Royal Regt. Lieut. P. Gravatt.
1 corporal, since dead.

WOUNDED.

H.M.'s 2d or Queen's Royal Regt. Capt. W. M. Lyster, severely.
ditto....ditto....ditto.... " T. Sealey, ditto
ditto....ditto.. .ditto....Lt.T.W.E. Holdsworth, do.
ditto....ditto....ditto.... " D. J. Dickinson, slightly.
ditto....ditto....ditto.... Adjt. J.E. Simmons, severely
H. M.'s 17th Regiment........Capt. L. C. Bonschier, do.
31st Regiment Bengal N. I.... " Lawrin, slightly.
ditto....ditto............Ensign Hopper, severely.

(Signed)   C. HAGART, Captain,
Acting Deputy-Adjutant-General, B. C.

State of the Corps engaged at the storming of Khelat, on the 13th November, 1839.—Under the Command of Major-General Willshire, C. B.

Camp at Khelat, 14th November, 1839.

Corps.	Major-Generals.	Brigadiers.	Aides-de-Camp.	Act.-Deputy-Adjt.-Genl.	Act.-Qr.-Mr.-Genl.	Dy.-Ass.-Qr.-Mr.-Genl.	Brigade-Majors.	Sub-Assist.-Comsy.-Gen.	Lieutenant-Colonels.	Majors.	Captains.	Lieutenants.	Ensigns.	Adjutants.	Quarter-Masters.	Surgeons.	Assistant-Surgeons.	Native Officers.	Sub-Conductors.	Serjeants.	Drummers.	Farriers.	Rank and File.
Staff	1	2	5	1	1	1	2	1	0	0	0	0	0	0	0	0	0	0	0	0	0	0	0
Detach. 3d Troop Horse Artillery	0	0	0	0	0	0	0	0	0	0	0	2	0	0	0	0	0	0	0	2	0	0	36
1st Troop of Cabool Artillery	0	0	0	0	0	0	0	0	0	0	0	1	0	0	0	0	0	0	0	8	1	1	58
H. M.'s 2nd or Queen's Roy. Regt.	0	0	0	0	0	0	0	0	0	1	3	7	1	1	0	0	0	0	0	31	10	0	290
H. M.'s 17th Regiment	0	0	0	0	0	0	0	0	1	2	4	13	2	0	1	1	0	0	0	29	9	0	336
31st Regt. Bengal Native Infantry	0	0	0	0	0	0	0	0	0	1	2	3	2	1	1	1	0	12	0	30	14	0	329
Total	1	2	5	1	1	1	2	1	1	4	9	26	5	2	2	2	0	12	0	100	34	1	1049

Note.—2 Ressalas of the Bengal Local Horse remained in charge of the baggage during the attack.

(Signed) C. HAGART, Captain,
Acting Deputy-Adjutant-General, Bombay Column, Army of the Indus.

APPENDIX.—KHELAT.

List of Beloche Sirdars killed in the Assault of Khelat, on the 13th November, 1839.

NAMES.	REMARKS.
Meer Mehrab Khan	Chief of Khelat.
Meer Wullee Mahomed	The Muengal Sirdar of Wudd.
Abdool Kurreem	Ruhsanee Sirdar.
Dan Kurreem	Shuhwanee Sirdar.
Mahomed Ruza	Nephew of the Vuzeer Mahomed Hossain.
Khysur Khan	Ahsehiee Sirdar
Dewan Bechah Mull	Financial Minister.
Noor Mahomed and Tajoo Mahomed.	Shahgassee Sirdars.

Prisoners

Mahomed Hussen. . Wuzzeer.
Moollah Ruheem Dad . Ex-Naib of Shawl.
With several others of inferior rank.

(Signed)   J. D. D. BEAN,
Political Agent.

(True copies.)

T. H. MADDOCK,
Offg. Secy. to Govt. of India with the Governor-General.

No. 7.

LONDON GAZETTE.

Downing Street, Aug. 12, 1839.

The Queen has been graciously pleased to nominate and appoint Lieut.-Gen. Sir John Keane, Knight Commander of the Most Honourable Order of the Bath, to be a Knight Grand Cross of the said Order.

Whitehall, Dec. 11, 1839.

The Queen has been pleased to direct letters patent to be passed under the Great Seal, granting the dignities of Baron and Earl of the United Kingdom of Great Britain and Ireland unto the Right Hon. George Lord Auckland, G. C. B. and the heirs male of his body lawfully begotten, by the names, styles, and titles of Baron Eden, of Norwood, in the county of Surrey, and Earl of Auckland.

The Queen has also been pleased to direct letters patent to be passed under the Great Seal, granting the dignity of a Baron of the United Kingdom of Great Britain and Ireland unto Lieut.-General Sir John Keane, G. C. B., and the heirs male of his body, lawfully begotten, by the name, style, and title of Baron Keane, of Ghuznee, in Affghanistan, and of Cappoquin in the county of Waterford.

The Queen has also been pleased to direct letters patent to be passed under the Great Seal, granting the dignity of a Baronet of the United Kingdom of Great Britain and Ireland unto the following gentlemen, and the heirs male of their bodies lawfully begotten, viz:—

William Hay Macnaghten, Esq., of the Civil Service of

the East India Company, on the Bengal Establishment, Envoy and Minister from the Government of India to His Majesty Shah Soojah-ool-Moolk ; and

Colonel Henry Pottinger, in the service of the East India Company, on the Bombay Establishment, Political Resident in Cutch.

The Queen has also been pleased to direct letters patent to be passed under the Great Seal of the United Kingdom of Great Britain and Ireland conferring the honor of Knighthood upon Lieutenant-Colonel Claude Martine Wade, of the Military Service of the East India Company, on the Bengal Establishment, Political Resident at Loodiana.

War Office, Dec., 13, 1839.

Brevet—The undermentioned commissions are to be dated 23rd July, 1839 : Colonel Robert Henry Sale, 13th Foot, to have the local rank of Major-General in Affghanistan.

To be Lieut.-Colonels in the Army—Major Charles Robert Cureton, 16th Dragoons; Major John Pennycuick, 17th Foot; Major Edward T. Tronson, 13th Foot ; Major Francis Dermot Daly, 4th light Dragoons ; Major Richard Carruthers, 2nd Foot; Major Geo. James M'Dowell, 16th Light Dragoons.

To be Majors in the Army—Capt. James Kershaw, 13th Foot; Capt. Thomas Sidney Powell, 6th Foot.

To be Lieut.-Colonels in the East Indies only—Major James Keith, of the Bombay N. I. (Deputy Adj.-Gen.) ; Major James Maclaren, of the Bengal N. I.; Major Peter L. Pew, of the Bengal Artil.; Major James C. Parsons, of the Bengal N. I. (Dep. Com.-Gen.) ; Major George Warren, Bengal European Reg.; Major Claude Martine Wade, Bengal N. I.; Major H. F. Salter, Bengal Cav,; Major David Cunynhame, Bombay Cavalry.

To be Majors in the East Indies only—Capt. Neil Campbell, Bombay N. I. (Deputy Quarter-master-Gen.); Captain George Thomson, of the Bengal Engineers; Capt. William Garden, Bengal N. I. (Dep. Quarter-master-Gen.);

Capt. John Hay, Bengal N. I.; Capt. John Lloyd, Bombay Artillery; Capt. Patrick Craigie, Bengal N. I. (Deputy Adj. Gen.); Captain Alexander C. Peat, Bombay Engineers; Capt. William Alexander, Bengal Cavalry.

To have the local rank of Major in Affghanistan—Lieut. Eldred Pottinger, Bombay Artillery.

Downing Street, Dec. 20, 1839.

The Queen has been graciously pleased to nominate and appoint—

Colonel Thomas Willshire, commanding the Bombay troop, and serving with the rank of Major-General in India:

Colonel Joseph Thackwell, commanding the Cavalry, and serving with the rank of Major General in India:

Colonel Robert Henry Sale, commanding the 13th Light Infantry, and serving with the rank of Major-General in Affghanistan—to be Knights Commanders of the Most Honourable Military order of the Bath.

Her Majesty has also been pleased to nominate and appoint the following officers in Her Majesty's service, to be Companions of the said Most Honourable Military Order of the Bath:

Lieut.-Colonel John Scott, of the 4th Light Dragoons.

Lieut.-Colonel William Persse, of the 16th Lancers.

Lieut.-Colonel William Croker of the 17th Foot.

Lieut.-Colonel Ronald Macdonald, of the 4th Foot, Deputy Adjutant General, Bombay.

Her Majesty has been further pleased to nominate and appoint the following officers, in the service of the East India Company, to be Companions of the Most Honourable Military Order of the Bath:—

Lieut.-Colonel Abraham Roberts, of the Bengal Native Infantry.

Lieut.-Colonel Thomas Stevenson, of the Bombay Artillery.

Lieut-Colonel Thomas Monteith, of the Bengal Native Infantry.

Lieut.-Colonel Hugh Massey Wheeler, of the Bengal Native Infantry.

Lieut.-Colonel Charles M. Carmichael Smyth, of the Bengal Native Cavalry.

Lieut.-Colonel Bentham Sandwith, of the Bombay Native Cavalry.

Lieut.-Colonel Foster Stalker, of the Bombay Native Infantry.

Lieut.-Colonel Claude Martine Wade, of the Bengal Native Infantry.

Major George Thomson, of the Bengal Engineers.

Major Eldred Pottinger, of the Bombay Artillery.

Downing Street, Jan., 21, 1840.

The Queen has been graciously pleased to nominate and appoint Major-General Sir Willoughby Cotton, Knight Commander of the most Honourable Order of the Bath, to be a Knight Grand Cross of the said Order.

OU TE

From Khelat to Soomeanee, via Nal, Beila and Lyaree.

Hours occupied.	Estimated Miles.	General Direction.	Remarks.
4	14	S. S. W.	Rodinjoe—small village: small stream of fine water; road excellent; about 5 miles from Khelat pass through a defile between hills, which could be easily ascended, or the pass turned; the rest of the road quite open; camel forage, the southern-wood shrub; scanty grass on the hills, must be plentiful in spring.
9	12	S. S. W.	Surmasing—two small wells close to the hills on the left of the valley, but more water said to be in the centre of the valley just opposite; road pretty good, but undulating and stony, skirting the hills the last 6 or 8 miles; no village or vegetation in the plain, except southern-wood shrub; scanty yellow grass on the hill sides.
	10	S. S. W.	1st Sohrab—small village: some trees and cultivation; stream of good wa-
13	36		

Hours occupied.	Estimated Miles.	General Direction.	REMARKS.
13	36		ter; road good, but rather stony, and undulating for about half way, till it leaves the hills for the centre of the valley; forage as above; no villages in the valley from Rodinjoe to this place.
	8	S. S. W.	Sohrab—a cluster of villages of that name, two other villages between the 1st Sohrab and these; considerable cultivation and some trees at each; forage as above.
			Here the roads separate to Gundava, Wudd, and Nal, and the valley terminates, which runs from the pass 5 miles from Khelat to this, (generally averaging from 15 to 20 miles in width), in a s. s. westerly direction. The villages at this season, are all deserted, the inhabitants descending to the Gundava plains for the winter.
6	24	S. S. W.	Small stream: no villages, but fields cultivated in spring; scanty camel forage, and grass in the hills; road bad, but quite practicable for guns, stony, and many small ascents and dips. No water or village on the road. The dry channels of several mountain streams which we passed, may contain water earlier in the season, but I could not clearly ascertain that point.
19	68		

s

Hours occupied.	Estimated Miles.	General Direction	Remarks.
19	68		
10	5	S. S. W.	Lakoora—signs of considerable cultivation, but no habitations; camel forage, and grass scanty; road good.
	10	S. S. W.	To the end of the Jewa valley—containing water and considerable cultivation, and some habitations, now deserted. Forage abundant; road for the first 3 miles through a range of hills (running to the westward), very rocky and will require some making for guns; latterly through the valley, very good.
	20	..	Parkoc—small village; lately destroyed by Mehrab Khan. Fine stream of water with turf on its banks. Camel and horse forage scanty; remains of cultivation and a few trees.
		S. E.	Ascend a rocky pass about 100 feet, requiring to be cleared for guns, and very steep; level road for about half a mile, then a descent of about 300 feet, very rocky and steep, requiring much labour to clear it for guns ; 3 miles to dry bed of river, running from northeast, rocky in some places; next ten miles the road is good, across a level plain to the site of a village, and remains of much cultivation, but could see no water; 3 miles further recross the same river (dry) running west; 3 miles more
29	103		

Hours occupied.	Estimated Miles.	General Direction.	Remarks.
29	103		reach Parkoo, road for the last 16 miles very good.
5	14	S. E.	Nal—a considerable village, and district containing several villages of the same name, occupying a wide and fertile valley, abundantly watered. Forage and supplies plentiful. Crossed a high range of hills (ascent about 500 feet and descent 1000) by a path quite impracticable for laden cattle of any description; the high road from Parkoo to Nal, said to be good (with no great ascent or descent) running through the hills considerably further to the right, and 5 or 6 miles longer than that by which I came.
10½	17	South.	Hamlets, and considerable cultivation, with abundant water, camel and grass forage. Road excellent; 6 miles, pass several villages, level plain, and clumps of tamarisk; 3 miles, stony plain, baubul jungle and tamarisk; 5 miles, level grass plain, with swamp on the left hand; for the last 2 miles, good water, hamlets and cultivation; for the next 3 miles, horse and camel forage, and water abundant.
	15	South.	Durruk (or Nal) River—cross the elbow of the river running from, and again going off to the left; no village; good stream of water; abundant camel fo-
44½	149		

Hours occupied.	Estimated Miles.	General Direction.	REMARKS.
44½	149		rage, but no grass. Road excellent; 6 miles over perfectly smooth plain, without a stone; nine miles undulating kunkur ground, with slight descent to the river, which appears to run parallel to the road (and about 2 miles distant) for some miles.
	14	South.	Durruk (or Nal) River—cross the same river, which here goes off to the westward, having run parellel to and about a mile from the road, since last touching it; no villages, but traces of cultivation here and there; abundant camel forage, but no grass; road perfectly smooth, without a stone.
8	14	South.	Bed of River—pools of water at the foot of the Oornach pass; camel forage, but no grass and no villages. For the first five or six miles, the Durruk river flanks the road about a mile off, then runs due west; road good the whole way, except for the last half mile, when there is a considerable ascent to the river, but perfectly practicable for guns without making.
	12	South	Bed of the Oornach River—small spring and pool of water; camel forage, but no grass, except just at the edge of the spring, enough for three or four horses. First five miles gradual ascent, road along dry water chan-
52½	189		

APPENDIX.—ROUTE. 259

Hours occupied.	Estimated Miles.	General Direction.	Remarks.
52½	189		nels, with firm, smooth, gravelly bottom, to the top of the Oornach Pass; descend 7 miles to the spring, gradually and by a similar and equally good road for the first 4 miles, till the road enters the dry bed of the Oornach river, which is much broken and very rocky.
18	7	S. E.	Oornach—village on the river a little to the right of the road, which leaves the river about 2 miles below the spring, and takes across hills to the left for 5 miles, when it re-crosses the river road; very rocky, would require clearing for guns.
	15	East.	Foot of Poorallee Pass—scanty supply of water to be obtained by digging in the sandy bottom of a ravine; no forage; road good, passing through the centre of a small valley, in which there are hamlets scattered and some cultivation, the Oornach river widening through it, is crossed three times, and then goes off due north (where it joins the Poorallee river I imagine), no water in it; the last 3 miles after leaving the valley, ascend considerably, and cross several ravines, bad for Artillery.
	2	East.	Top of Poorallee Pass—From water ravine, the road winds along the sides of hills and ravines only wide enough
70½	213		

Hours occupied	Estimated Miles.	General Direction.	Remarks.
70½	213		
			for one animal to pass at a time, and not capable of being easily widened; ascent gradual.
	1	East.*	To bottom of Pass—descent exceedingly abrupt, and rocky at one time, confined some distance between perpendicular rocks, and barely wide enough for a laden camel to pass. Here, immense labour would be required to widen it sufficiently for guns,—I saw no means of turning it; the remainder of the descent is so abrupt as to be impracticable for guns, and it could not easily, if at all, be improved; water is seen at the bottom of a deep glen a little off the road, but it could not easily be go at.
	6	East.	Springs of water, but scanty, at the bottom of a ravine; road pretty good, but there are three deep ravines to cross; grass round the springs sufficient for half a dozen horses; no other horse forage; plenty of baubul jungle and tamarisk for camels; no villages to be seen from the top of the Pass as far as the eye could reach; nothing but a succession of mountains on all sides.
7	5	S. E.	Top of another range,—road good, and ascent gradual, generally along water channels, with firm sandy bottoms no water.
77½	225		

Hours occupied.	Estimated Miles.	General Direction.	REMARKS.
77¼	225		
	15	S. E.	Gradual descent by similar roads; very good, but generally confined by high mountains or precipitous rocks, to some springs oozing from the sandy bottom of a deep ravine; no space for encamping the smallest force near the water, but ample shelter would be afforded by the high rocks on both sides. For some distance above and below the water, no forage exists for horses; ample tamarisk, &c., for camels. No traces of human habitation anywhere in the neighbourhood of this day's route.
9½	10	S. E.	Road, still along water channels, and confined by hills and rocks, but a wide and firm gravel road, to some small brackish springs; no habitations; camel forage.
	7	S. E.	Cross the Poorallee River—a fine stream; camel and horse forage; no habitation; river running due south.
	12	South.	Chandra—follow the left bank of the river till opposite to the village, cross to it; abundance of forage and supplies; the road generally good, but stony and undulating; the bed of the river very wide and stony; villages and cultivation on the bank for the last six miles.
10½	12	South.	Beila (Beilou)—cross the Poorallee and along its stony bed for the first 3 miles, then good road to the town, large
97⅓	281		

Hours occupied.	Estimated Miles.	General Direction.	Remarks.
97½	281		place; ample supplies, and forage for camels and horses.
	13	South.	Touch an elbow of the Poorallee river; no village; horse and camel forage; road good; country perfectly level; several small hamlets passed.
	15	South.	Cross Poorallee river—considerable stream; grass and tamarisk abundant, no village, and scarcely any habitations passed on the road; road excellent, and perfectly smooth.
14	12	South.	An artificial bund, confining a considerable extent of water; hamlets in the vicinity; forage abundant.
	10	South.	Lyarsa—large village; first 4 miles through thick jungle; road in some parts very uneven, and at others through heavy sand.
	24	E. S. E.	Sonmeanee—road excellent, except the last 4 miles through deep sand. The Poorallee and its branches marked in the map, between Lyaree and Sonmeanee, are not perceptible, but a considerable river of that name empties itself into the bay off the eastern side of the town, and I presume it has no other outlets.
111½	355		

N. B.—The distances are computed by the pace of the ambling ponies and camels we rode, averaging from two and a half to five miles per hour, according to the nature of the road. The direction is judged by the sun during the day, and moon and stars at night. Both forage and water more scarce at this season, than any other period of the year.

(Signed)   J. OUTRAM, Capt.

www.ingramcontent.com/pod-product-compliance
Lightning Source LLC
Chambersburg PA
CBHW071815230426
43670CB00013B/2461